SIDEWALKS IN THE KINGDOM

The Christian Practice of Everyday Life

David S. Cunningham
and William T. Cavanaugh, series editors

This series seeks to present specifically Christian perspectives on some of the most prevalent contemporary practices of everyday life. It is intended for a broad audience—including clergy, interested laypeople, and students. The books in this series are motivated by the conviction that, in the contemporary context, Christians must actively demonstrate that their allegiance to the God of Jesus Christ always takes priority over secular structures that compete for our loyalty—including the state, the market, race, class, gender, and other functional idolatries. The books in this series will examine these competing allegiances as they play themselves out in particular day-to-day practices, and will provide concrete descriptions of how the Christian faith might play a more formative role in our everyday lives.

The Christian Practice of Everyday Life series is an initiative of The Ekklesia Project, an ecumenical gathering of pastors, theologians, and lay leaders committed to helping the church recall its status as the distinctive, real-world community dedicated to the priorities and practices of Jesus Christ and to the inbreaking Kingdom of God. (For more information on The Ekklesia Project, see <www.ekklesiaproject.org>.)

ERIC O. JACOBSEN

SIDEWALKS IN THE KINGDOM

New Urbanism and the Christian Faith

THE CHRISTIAN PRACTICE
OF EVERYDAY LIFE Series

Brazos Press
A Division of Baker Book House Co
Grand Rapids, Michigan 49516

Published by Brazos Press
a division of Baker Book House Company
P.O. Box 6287, Grand Rapids, MI 49516-6287
http://www.brazospress.com

Printed in the United States of America

Library of Congress Cataloging-in-Publication Data

Jacobsen, Eric O.
    Sidewalks in the Kingdom : new urbanism and the Christian faith / Eric O. Jacobsen.
        p.   cm. — (The Christian practice of everyday life) Includes bibliographical references.
    ISBN 1-58743-057-6
    1. Cities and towns—Religious aspects—Christianity. 2. Cities and towns—United States. I. Title. II. Series
    BR115.C45J33 2003
    277.3′083′091732—dc21   2002154569

Scripture is taken from the New Revised Standard Version of the Bible, copyright 1989 by the Division of Christian Education of the National Council of the Churches of Christ in the USA. Used by permission.

Parts of chapter 4 were previously published as "Learning to See Our Cities" in *Radix* 29.1 (2002): 12–15, 26.

Contents

Acknowledgments

I would like to thank my father Conrad Jacobsen for modeling a life of disciplined study and my mother Judi Jacobsen for her constant cheerleading; my father-in-law Earl Palmer for suggesting that I start writing and my mother-in-law Shirley Palmer who also risked writing out of her passion; Eugene Peterson for enduring the first draft and encouraging me the whole way; Daniel Kemmis for igniting in me a fire for citizenship; Albert Borgmann for modeling a high standard of Christian scholarship; Lynn Schreuder for giving me words for what I was seeing; Jack and Kelly Oats for being my first converts and for clipping countless articles; Peter Lambros for being up past midnight as often as I—and always ready for a walk; David Cunningham and Bill Cavanaugh for seeing strong possibilities for a book; Rodney Clapp for caring about the ideas independently of the book project; the Brazos Press staff for treating me like a "real" author; the 9:30 Adult Ed class for correcting some glaring errors; the First Presbyterian Church of Missoula for some seed money to get started and the Lilly Foundation for a reason to get finished; and the great city of Missoula Montana for giving me more than I could ever give back.

And I would especially like to thank Katherine, Peter, Emma, and my beloved wife Liz, without whom I would only be a noisy gong.

Foreword

In the Christian imagination, where you live gets equal billing with what you believe. Geography and theology are biblical bedfellows. Everything that the creator God does, and therefore everything that we do, since we are his creatures and can hardly do anything in any other way, is in *place*. All living is local—this land, this neighborhood, these trees and streets and houses, this work, these shops and markets.

This is, of course, obvious, but all the same it needs saying—sometimes requiring a raised voice. I have spent an adult lifetime with the assigned task of guiding men and women into living out the Christian faith in the place in which they raise their children and work for a living, go fishing and play golf, buy their groceries and park their cars. In the course of this work, I find that cultivating a sense of place as the exclusive and irreplaceable setting for following Jesus is even more difficult than persuading men and woman of the truth of the message of Jesus. Why is it easier for me to believe in the holy (because God inspired it) truth of John 3:16 than the holy (because God made it) ground at 579 Apricot Lane where I live?

One of the seductions that continues to bedevil Christian obedience is the construction of utopias, whether in fact or fantasy, ideal places where we can live the good and blessed and righteous life without inhibition or interference. The imagining and attempted construction of utopias is an old habit of our kind. Sometimes we attempt it politically in communities, sometimes socially in communes, sometimes religiously in churches. It never comes to anything but grief. Meanwhile that place we actually are is dismissed or demeaned as inadequate for serious living to the glory of God. But utopia is literally "no-place." We can only live our lives in actual place, not imagined or fantasized or artificially fashioned places.

A favorite story of mine, one that has held me fast to my place several times, is of Gregory of Nyssa who lived in Cappadocia (a region in modern Turkey) in the fourth century. His older brother, a bishop, arranged for him to be appointed bishop of the small and obscure and unimportant town of Nyssa (A.D. 371) Gregory objected; he didn't want to be stuck in such an out-of-the-way place. But his brother told him that he didn't want

9

Gregory to obtain distinction from his church but rather to confer distinction upon it. Gregory went to where he was placed and stayed there. His lifetime of work in that place, a backwater community, continues to be a major invigorating influence in the Christian church worldwide.

Our Scriptures that bring us the story of our salvation ground us in place. Everywhere they insist on this grounding. Everything that is critically important to us takes place on the ground. Mountains and valleys, towns and cities, regions and countries: Haran, Ur, Canaan, Hebron, Sodom, Machpelah, Bethel, Bethlehem, Jerusalem, Samaria, Tekoa, Nazareth, Capernaum, Mt. Sinai, Mt. Of Olives, Mt. Gilboah, Mt. Hermon, Ceasarea, Gath, Ashkelon, Michmash, Gibeon, Azekah, Jericho, Chorizan, Bethsaida, Emmaus, the Valley of Jezreel, the Kidron Valley, the Brook of Besor, Anathoth. Big cities and small towns. Famous landmarks and unvisited obscurities. People who want God or religion as an escape from their place because it is difficult (or maybe just mundane), don't find this much to their liking. But there it is—there's no getting around it. But to the man or woman wanting *more* reality, not less, this insistence that all genuine life, life that is embraced in God's work of salvation, is *grounded,* is good news indeed.

It is the passion of Eric Jacobsen to bring us into an attentive consideration of the place where we live and get us to explore the ways in which the place itself with its many dimensions is integral to the gospel in the way we live. This book is important gospel work. We are used to having natural places, our mountains and rivers, appreciated as sacred places. And we are used to having secularized and problem-ridden cities targeted as places for critical and sometimes dramatic missions. But we aren't used to this, this pastor who sees and helps us to see these ordinary places where so many of us live as gift-places, as holy sites. If we hadn't already noticed the enormous significance of where we are and how critical it is to live in ways that deepen and extend God's gift of community we certainly will as we read the pages of *Sidewalks in the Kingdom.*

What we often consider to be the concerns of religion—ideas, truths, prayers, promises, beliefs—are never permitted to have a life of their own apart from particular persons and actual places. Biblical religion has a low tolerance for "great ideas" or "sublime truths" or "inspirational thoughts" apart from the places in which they occur. God's great love and purposes for us are worked out in the messes in our kitchens and backyards, in storms and sins, blue skies, daily work, working with us as we are and not as we should be, and where we are, on "sidewalks in the kingdom," and not where we would like to be.

Eugene J. Peterson
Professor Emeritus of Spiritual Theology
Regent College

Introduction
A Trip to Bernice's

But seek the welfare of the city where I have sent you into exile, and pray to the LORD on its behalf, for in its welfare you will find your welfare.

Jeremiah 29:7

There have been times, not least the time of the birth of Athenian democracy, when most of the people who thought and wrote about human wholeness concluded that no one could be a whole human being, nor achieve the satisfactions of such wholeness, without participating fully in citizenship.

Daniel Kemmis, The Good City and the Good Life

■ It's Tuesday morning and time for my weekly meeting with Jack—the senior pastor of our church. It's a beautiful morning, so I suggest that rather than meet in one of our offices, we have our meeting at Bernice's— one of the local coffee shops. We grab our coats and soon are crunching through the fall leaves on the church lawn on our way to the sidewalk along 5th Street.

Just before Big Dipper Ice Cream, we turn down Hazel and head north toward the river. Along the two blocks of Hazel Street, we pass by three residential houses, two apartment buildings, two churches, a microbrewery, a bakery, and a photography studio. Bernice's occupies the site of the historic Knowles Building, which was designed in 1905 by the prominent Missoula architect A. J. Gibson. Gibson, a former member of our church, is somewhat of a local legend due to his work in designing the county courthouse, Main Hall at the university, and the central high school, as well as our own church sanctuary. Once we are inside the door of Bernice's, our senses are filled with the smell of fresh-baked pastries and strong coffee. As we wait in line, our eyes are drawn to the beautifully restored brickwork and ceiling tiles as we casually observe the work of this week's featured artist displayed on the walls.

After we get our coffee, we notice that almost every table is filled. There are students studying, workers in Carhardt jeans having their morning break, moms and dads with young children, and a local politician planning her campaign strategy. We spot two open chairs and ask the others at the table if they wouldn't mind us joining them. Once settled, we commence with our regular pastoral staff meeting, oblivious to the gentle hum of conversation and activity going on all around us. We end with prayer and head out the door on our way back to church. Just across the street, we see a line beginning to form outside of the Missoula Food Bank and are reminded that it is near the end of the month and that wallets are starting to get a little thin for some of our residents. And we make it back to church just in time for the general staff meeting, where we discuss our plans for ministry in Missoula.

A trip to Bernice's with Jack or anyone from our church family seems so ordinary to me that I hardly notice it in the scope of my day. However, if our church were not in a city—or even if our church were in a different part of the city—this particular kind of experience would not have been possible. And it's not too hard to imagine a scenario in which our church community would cease to be in the city. Our congregation recently considered a proposal that, had it been accepted, would have radically altered our interaction with the surrounding environment by effectively taking us out of the city.

The proposal came about as a possible solution to two ongoing problems that we have with our current site. Our buildings are too small for our growing congregation, and we don't have sufficient parking. Being hemmed in by two busy arterial streets limits our options when it comes to solving these problems. The proposal that we contemplated as a congregation, then, was to move our church to Reserve Street—a rapidly developing commercial area on the fringe of the city. This would have allowed our building and parking needs to be solved much more inexpensively than they could be in our current location. We could have started from the ground up and designed a facility optimally suited to meet our needs.

On the other hand, if we were to make this move, we would be choosing, consciously or unconsciously, a suburban rather than an urban model for development, which would, in turn, place a different kind of limitation on our future ministry. Whatever specific size or type of building we would construct, we would ultimately end up with some kind of a large, monolithic building surrounded by an ocean of parking, just like every other building on Reserve Street. We would be about a half a mile from any other business and would not be connected with sidewalks for easy walking. If Jack and I wanted to get coffee for a meeting, we would have to drive some distance from our church and would not have any opportunity for personally greeting any of our commercial or residential neighbors.

Conversely, anyone who wanted to come to our church would have to either drive there themselves or be driven there by someone else. Those without access to a car—like many of our college students or elderly members—would not be able to get here at all. Aesthetically, every building within view of our site would have been built within the same decade as ours, with very little architectural style or integration with the surrounding environment, and we would be hard-pressed to see any details of construction that would suggest a sense of quality in workmanship.

This is not to say that such a move would have been catastrophic for our church. There would have been many advantages to adopting this new site, and there is a great need for ministry on the growing edges of our city. My point is that there are implications for a church and its ministry that are wider and more far-reaching than might be seen through eyes that see parking and square-footage needs exclusively. The location of a church—and the character of its surrounding context—can have a major impact on the kind of ministry that can be done in a particular community. What we preserved by staying at our current site is the possibility of doing ministry in a city.

Without really being aware of it, Jack and I had experienced—in our short meeting—six markers that are distinctive of the city. We shared *public spaces* with other residents of our community by using the sidewalk and by meeting in a coffee shop. We were able to walk rather than drive to our meeting because of our *mixed-use* neighborhood, which allows residential and commercial buildings to coexist. We enjoyed the nonessential *beauty* in the quality of a locally designed and built structure as well as in the artist's work on its walls. We saw some of the results of a *local economy* as workers recycled their wages at a locally owned establishment. Our hearts were burdened with the presence of *strangers* at the food bank who have needs beyond their resources. And we saw friends and minicoalitions gathering around tables at Bernice's, who found one another through the *critical mass* of the city.

Most of these markers exist or have existed in locations around the world that we call cities. However, due to the aggregate effect of many decisions like the one we contemplated as a church, our cities are becoming distinctly less city-like. Culturally, we are losing a sense of what it means to function within the context of a city and in many cases have slipped into radically different models of existence without even realizing it.

Over the past decade or so, there has been a growing awareness of this problem and a concerted effort to preserve and restore many of these markers of the city to our historic urban places as well as to our newer developments. This trend has been dubbed New Urbanism and has attracted an eclectic mix of architects, builders, city planners, and even sociologists to its front lines. New Urbanism has inspired a number of other movements, including smart growth in government circles, and Traditional Neighborhood Design among developers. However, to most Christians, the idea of urban planning seems as relevant to faith as the current additions to the American Kennel Association's list of approved dog breeds—interesting to some, but certainly not vital to faith. Despite the mounting corpus of secular literature on the subject and the rising interest in New Urbanism, Christians as a distinct group have stayed out of this conversation.

It's not as if we have no interest in the city. There are numerous Christian books on the city and about urban ministry. It's just that as Christians, we have tended to treat the city as a problem to be solved or a burden to be borne. The city is largely seen as an abstract place where humanity is gathered in the greatest concentration and therefore where the problems and needs of humans are most obvious and pressing. We have not, as our secular contemporaries are beginning to do, taken seriously the physical form or context of existing cities as a viable model for our shared community life. Nor have we seen in our historic cities constructive models for new developments.

I became interested in the city and urban planning in, ironically, a place that seems to just barely qualify as a city in terms of population. Though I have spent most of my life in the urban locations of Seattle and the San Francisco Bay area, I am now a pastor in Missoula, Montana. Missoula is a city with a population of just over 65,000 that sits at about 3,000 feet in the heart of the Rocky Mountains. The Clark Fork River cuts through the center of town and joins the Blackfoot and Bitterroot rivers, providing a physical link with the Pacific Ocean. Missoula is also the home of the University of Montana—which on one side touches 40,000 acres of untamed wilderness, and on the other, a whole world of ideas and cultures through its classrooms, professors, and student body.

There are a lot of reasons that my wife and I chose to come to Missoula, not the least of which was that this just seemed like a good place for us to start our family. And it seems that we are not alone in choosing Missoula—lots of people are opting to live here. Even though the city's job market is extremely poor, people are enduring severe pay cuts to come and be part of this community. Missoula is not the proverbial small town where everyone knows everyone else. And it is not a megalopolis like Atlanta or Houston, where traffic and sprawl have created more of an urban caricature than an actual living and breathing city. Missoula is a city with a mixed and interesting population where life is lived on a human scale. People have chosen to come to Missoula, looking for something that we've lost in our culture. And I believe that this something might be the notion of a city.

I first became aware of this concept through reading *The Good City and the Good Life*, written by Missoula's former mayor Daniel Kemmis. In this book, Kemmis calls our attention away from the national political scene—which is making us increasingly jaded as citizens—to our cities and the local issues that are being addressed on a human scale. Kemmis is not a theologian, but his work is filled with terms and descriptions that are really best categorized as theological. Kemmis reminds us that "what makes a city a good city is not its capacity to distract, but the way in which it creates presence."[1] Also, "the city in grace . . . answers to a deep longing for a spiritual dimension in public life."[2] And finally, "I was reminded of how often I saw scenes like this at the market, and it occurred to me that this had become, in fact, a kind of sacrament."[3]

Reading words like *presence, grace,* and *sacrament* in a book about the city made me realize that there is potentially a lot more theological interest in city planning than I had previously understood. I met with Kemmis to discuss his ideas, and he introduced me to a slew of writers who had also been rediscovering something very valuable in our cities, authors like Jane Jacobs, who forty years ago prophesied the inherent perils of our suburban flight in her landmark book *The Death and Life of Great American Cities*.[4] And more recently James Howard Kunstler, whose two books *The Geography of Nowhere* and *Home from Nowhere* powerfully document the spiritual bankruptcy of most of our postwar building efforts.[5] And there are a host of others, like Peter Katz, who helped launch the Congress for the New Urbanism and served as its first director, and Richard Moe and Carter Wilkie, who have been instrumental in the historic preservation movement.[6]

In the works of these secular authors, I found convergent themes of longing for community, joy, beauty, place, connection with our past, and meaning. I found all sorts of ideas and issues within this body of literature in which the church community has also been very much interested. But in each of the Christian books that I consulted, the city, whether vilified or exalted, was treated as an abstraction. The city was a place of deep human need or sometimes a place of divine possibility, but never a place with sidewalks or plazas.

This is most unfortunate, because we of all people have a deep history of interest in the city, rooted in our biblical tradition. Long before Jane Jacobs, Daniel Kemmis, Peter Katz, and James Howard Kunstler began envisioning something inherently redeemable in our cities, John the evangelist was engaged in his own form of urban visioning.[7] When John, exiled on Patmos, is given a picture of our redeemed state, he does not see Eden restored in some kind of an agrarian utopia; nor does he see the American ideal of a single-family detached house surrounded by a huge yard for every inhabitant of the kingdom. What he sees is a city—New Jerusalem descending from heaven onto earth.

And because a city is what John sees, Christians must take this vision seriously and not replace it with our own visions of the ideal human environment. For the past two decades, Christians have been tempted in this direction. We have been abandoning our strategic locations within city cores and traditional neighborhoods, and we have tried to create for ourselves a new kind of society in the form of suburban megachurches. And as individual Christians, we have marched right along with the rest of our culture and moved our homes outside of the urban core into the sanitized world of the suburbs. Even when we have not participated directly in this radical shift, we have come to view the particularities of functioning in the midst of the city (restricted parking, unsympathetic neighbors, and pushy transients) as inconveniences rather than as opportunities for ministry.

But some Christians and some churches have hung in there and are continuing to be a part of the urban fabric in historic cities and traditional neighborhoods. Whether they have done so on purpose or inadvertently doesn't ultimately matter. They are continuing to work out their calling to ministry in the midst of the (sometimes messy) confines of the city. And this, I believe, has great significance for the building up of the kingdom and the healing of our culture.

Clearly there are profound problems within our cities, and in many cases the city has become a burden to be borne. And our cities require not only presence, but targeted mission efforts. Thankfully there are Christians who have been specially convicted by these problems and are on the forefront of the effort to mend our broken cities. However, all Christians must resist the temptation to take an eraser to our cities—to start over and find new and "improved" ways of relating to one another. We can start over only by ignoring our biblical tradition. Like it or not, when Christ wanted to show John a picture of what our redeemed life was going to look like, he showed him a city. We would do well to consider the specific context of our cities as we consider the various forms of ministry to which Christ may be calling us.

Part 1

Thinking about Our Cities

For my thoughts are not your thoughts, nor are your ways my ways, says the LORD. For as the heavens are higher than the earth, so are my ways higher than your ways and my thoughts than your thoughts.

Isaiah 55:8–9

■ "The fear of the LORD is the beginning of wisdom" (Psalm 111:10). This means that, as Christians, we look to God and not to ourselves as the ultimate source of truth. We go to Scripture, we pray, and we seek out the counsel of our Christian community to shape our understanding of the world. We try to recognize the influence of our feelings, our culture, or our immediate circumstances in the shaping of our worldview, but we do not give these things authoritative status.

Unfortunately, if we were to take a hard look at how Christians in this country have come to view their cities, we would have to conclude that our views have not necessarily been shaped by the Bible, prayer, or meaningful discussions among fellow Christians. It might be more accurate to say that the fear of cities, or the fear of one another, or possibly the love of convenience has been the actual basis of much of our current perceptions about the city. Not surprisingly, our perceptions have tended to be largely negative. We have moved our homes and our congregations to the very fringes of our historic cities or to suburban enclaves. And we have learned to speak of cities exclusively as places for rescue missions rather than as places to live, work, worship, or play.

In this next section, we will try to trace the origin of this antiurban bias in our culture in general and among Christians in particular. Then we will attempt to approach the Bible with fresh eyes in order to develop a theology of the city from Genesis to Revelation. This biblical foundation will, then, provide a background for a specific analysis of the features of the city, which will follow.

Broken Promises: Sprawl and the American Experience

Can any idols of the nations bring rain? Or can the heavens give showers? Is it not you, O LORD our God? We set our hope on you, for it is you who do all this.

Jeremiah 14:22

If anything, there appears to be an inverse relationship between our growing obsession with the home as a totem object and the disintegration of families that has become the chief social phenomenon of our time. We worship this idealized container for family life, and yet it turns out that the family cannot be sustained without the larger container of community life.

James Howard Kunstler, *Home from Nowhere*

 Do You Know the Way to San Jose?: The False Promise of Sprawl

One of my earliest childhood memories is of sitting at the breakfast table with my mom, listening to the AM radio after everyone else had left for school. One song I remember distinctly from that morning tradition was Dionne Warwick's "Do You Know the Way to San Jose?" This song tells the story of a woman who is disillusioned with the big city of Los Angeles and wants to get back to San Jose, where everything is peaceful, beautiful, and spacious. I remember this song because it evoked such vivid images in my mind. It impressed upon me both that the big city was dirty and impersonal and that there existed idyllic enclaves with names like San Jose, where one could escape all of the city's problems and find fulfillment and meaning. It was an odd impression in some ways, because Seattle—the city in which I actually resided—was a fairly pleasant and nurturing place, from which I had never really harbored any fantasies of escape. So at the same time, the song evoked a suspicion of a city I had never visited and painted an idealized picture of escape from that place and others like it.

This impression lasted within me until I actually had the occasion to visit San Jose. I do not remember the exact date of my first encounter with that city, but I had seen San Jose on the map of northern California many times. It is located on Highway 880, somewhere between Berkeley and Santa Cruz. I know this because I attended college in Berkeley and spent a summer as a camp counselor in the mountains of Santa Cruz. However, it took a couple of times driving this particular stretch of road before I realized that I had encountered the San Jose of my childhood imagination.

What I observed on that highway was nothing like the image that had formed in my head from the song. In fact, nothing on that stretch of highway evoked a distinct impression of a city, a town, or any kind of defined human community. The view from the highway (where you could see past the concrete sound barrier) consisted of an unbroken sea of strip malls and housing developments. And on the unfortunate trips where I needed to actually exit the freeway for some reason or another, I was utterly disoriented by the lack of architectural cues that might direct me to the center of town or the commercial hub. It was so ugly and so lacking in any evidence of human community that I could not fathom what Los Angeles must have been like to make this place appear idyllic in contrast.

Now, it must be acknowledged that a lot of time had passed between when that song was written and my ill-fated voyages through this civic wasteland. Perhaps there was a time when San Jose was the perfect antidote to the problems of Los Angeles. But if it was, it had certainly taken a turn for the worse by the time I visited it. San Jose has since become for me a symbol of the kinds of poor decisions that are being made in this country regarding our human habitation. And it has served as a warning about where we are heading if we don't take a hard look at the assumptions and motivations behind these decisions.

■ False Gods and the American Experience

It is important to note that we have not been backed into sprawl and standardization as the dominant mode of development because of poverty, national crisis, or other limiting factors. Instead, we have boldly and confidently marched toward these unsatisfying arrangements with no one to blame but ourselves. We have done so, I believe, because we have been worshiping false gods in the name of American values.

These gods go by the names of individualism, independence, and freedom, but they take many forms in our daily experience. In this chapter, we will discover that these gods are beset by the same weakness of all false idols; namely, they consistently fail to deliver what they promise. We will suggest biblical values related to but not synonymous with these false gods that offer a more hopeful direction for our aspirations.

Individualism

Individualism can be defined as "the doctrine that the interests of the individual should take precedence over the interests of the state or social group."[1] Individualism has been an important value in this country since its very inception. The first immigrants to this country came looking for freedom to worship God according to their individual conscience and not according to state directive. Individualism provides the basis for our founding documents, with the Declaration of Independence asserting each person's right to "life, liberty, and the pursuit of happiness." This value was a foundational idea for this country, and it has not been diluted as it has been handed down from generation to generation.

Limitations on individualism are tolerated only in cases where the exercise of your individual rights impinges on my freedom to exercise mine. For example, a city ordinance that restricts noise levels after a certain hour at night is acceptable because your right to make noise is tempered by my right to have a peaceful night's sleep. On the other hand, a city ordinance restricting the palette of color from which you can choose your house paint is unacceptable (to our dominant mode of thinking) because the color of your house in no way limits my freedom to choose the color of my house. The value placed on individualism in this country is not necessarily limited to the private citizen but seems to apply to commercial entities as well. If Wal-Mart wants to open a store in our city, or if a developer wants to erect a massive tract home development on the outskirts of the city, any attempt to block or restrict the plans is seen to be authoritarian and thus unacceptable.

Individualism, theologically considered, may not be altogether bad. But our militant devotion to this value can easily become for us a false god and a distraction from the will of God for our lives. God is not overly concerned with our individual rights and preferences, but rather wants us to submit these things to himself and to one another out of love. Of course, God does care for us deeply as individuals. One of the great mysteries of the Christian faith is that the more we submit our will to the will of God, the more we become uniquely ourselves.

This leads us to the other problem with individualism—at least in the form that we have come to understand it. Individualism simply does not deliver what it promises. If a visitor to the United States were to view the acres and acres of identical tract home developments that we build and occupy year after year, do you think he or she would ever guess that our country was founded on a deep reverence for individualism? Imagine that same person on a tour of American cities including such diverse locations as Atlanta, Houston, and Seattle, seeing the same chain retail stores taking over in each and every location until it becomes difficult to distinguish one place from the other? Would the person not assume that this is a state-run economy wherein the individual good is valued much less than the collective?

Granted, we could explain to our visitor the indisputable fact that virtually every purchase made at the chain retail store and every purchase of a home in the tract development resulted from individual choice. But we would also have to concede that in many cases the choices of the personal consumer had been overshadowed by the choices of the giant corporation. We would have to explain that if people did happen to want an individually designed home or to shop somewhere besides the large chain retailer, they would find their options severely limited. Large corporations and major developers have limited the options available to the individual consumer by driving out the competition.

This is not initially perceived as a limit on our individual freedom, because in the short term we have more choices and lower prices. But in the long run, our options can become considerably more limited. We are hard-wired to resist governmental intervention in these kinds of situations, but the fact of the matter is that sometimes we need the government to balance out the corporations' freedom in order to preserve the consumers' freedom.

When Jesus was in the midst of a very large crowd, he surprised his disciples by asking "Who touched my clothes?" and took the time to notice one particular woman who was desperate for an encounter with him.[2] Jesus encountered people one at a time, as individuals, and he took a different approach with each person to whom he ministered. He healed one person with mud and spittle and another with a simple command. And he taught that God has every single one of the hairs on our heads numbered. Jesus honored and preserved the individual identity of people through his relationship with them and his compassion toward them.

When we compare Jesus' approach to ministry to our increasingly standardized housing and retail choices, he seems to have a lot more respect for the individual than our narrow version of consumer individualism seems to offer. And so developing a healthy respect for the individual in our building practices and in our consumer choices might actually better reflect the Christian values to which we subscribe. Consider the comments the Dutch theologian Abraham Kuyper made over one hundred years ago about standardized housing in America:

> There is not a gable to be seen which in any way violates the absolute symmetry to which door and window, cornice and roof window, have been fitted. Precisely those straight streets and rectangular corners, those utterly level gables and standardized houses make the modern outgrowths of our cities fatally exhausting and boring. You have to number the streets and count them out so as not to get lost in so featureless a collection of houses.[3]

Contrast his impressions of individually built homes in Holland:

> You can immediately tell that no shoddy, money-hungry developer threw up that line of houses but that every dwelling is the fulfillment of a personal dream, the precious product of quiet thrift, based on a personal plan and built slowly from the ground up. Those tufted, tiered, triangular, and shuttered gables were not symmetrically measured with a level but reflected every one of them the thinking of a human being, the whimsicality of a somewhat overconfident human heart.[4]

Perhaps Kuyper's sense of the dehumanizing tendencies implicit in standardized housing and his clear preference for individual expression provide a model for how we might develop a more comprehensive Christian critique of our current housing and retail practices.

Independence

Unlike individualism, which was a founding principle in this country, independence is a value that seems to have grown up more organically in our national experience. Whereas individualism is focused on limiting the institutional forces that might impinge on the individual's freedom, independence focuses on the individual's ability to survive and thrive on his or her own resources. Independence has been idealized in the image

23

of the American cowboy who rides into town alone, is silently heroic in the face of difficult circumstances, and then rides off into the sunset alone.

This country's love affair with the car has been fueled largely by our preoccupation with independence. The car allows us to do what we want, when we want, irrespective of distance or obstacle. It seems to be the perfect venue for the quintessential American experience and has over the years become the dominant feature of our daily lives. However, what we have failed to realize after almost a century of car culture is that the cumulative effect of our use of this machine has limited its ability to deliver on its promise.

Cars have allowed us to spread out our living patterns significantly. Historically, cities have had a natural limit set by how far people could comfortably walk from place to place. Then, with the development of streetcars, settlement spread in conjunction with the streetcar tracks. Slowly, with the onset of the automobile, the limits on sprawl were all but obliterated. As cars freed up drivers to live, work, shop, and play between farther and farther distances, these great distances became a fixed part of the landscape, making the car necessary for full participation in society. The shift has been subtle, but unmistakable, as we've moved from thinking of the car as a convenience to considering it a necessity.

This arrangement, at best, grants independence to one particular segment of our population while leaving many out. Youth who are too young too drive are completely dependent upon their parents to get them from place to place. There once was a time when a young person could walk to the corner store to get a treat, walk to the local park for baseball practice, and even walk to school. Now many kids need to be driven to each of these settings—putting additional pressure on parents, who must serve as their chauffeurs.

Historically, when a person turned eighteen in this country he or she would be seen to have gained full participation in our culture because of his or her right to vote. But in terms of true access to participation in our culture, voting has been trumped by access to a car and a driver's license. Almost every young person I know is far more excited about turning fifteen (or sixteen) and being able to drive to school, to practice, and to the mall than about turning eighteen and getting a chance to cast a vote in an election that is not perceived to have much bearing on day-to-day life.

When people get too old to drive, they suffer a fate similar to our children's. They must be driven to doctor's appointments, on shopping trips, or to visit their family. The practice of putting the elderly into retirement homes is a relatively recent phenomenon and is yet another outgrowth of our sprawling car culture:

Prior to 1950, there were few if any retirement communities in the United States; they did not exist because they were not needed. The elderly would almost always stay in their old neighborhoods after retiring. Once they lost their ability to drive, they could still maintain a viable lifestyle by walking, even if slowly.[5]

This generational segregation is deeply damaging to the fabric of our society:

> The segregation of the old causes the same rift inside each individual life; as old people pass into old age communities their ties with their own past become unacknowledged, lost, and therefore broken. Their youth is no longer alive in their old age—the two become dissociated; their lives are cut in two.[6]

Our love for the car has clearly severed important ties to both the young and the elderly in our midst. And we have not gained much in return.

There are also those who are disabled and cannot drive a car, as well as those who cannot afford a car, who are left behind in our current auto culture. And more and more, even those who have cars and can drive are finding diminishing returns for their independence as we continue to build everything around the needs of the car. Traffic has gotten so bad that even those who can drive are finding restrictions on their mobility around every corner.

Again, it's ironic that our love for independence has led us to create dependent classes among our citizenry. It appears that by focusing our aspiration for independence on one particular group within our culture, we have not only left many other groups in highly dependent situations, but we have also reached a saturation point where everyone's independence is being curtailed. Anyone who has missed an important event because of a traffic jam will have felt this reality. In short, we have found independence to be unable to deliver its seductive promise. Our experience with the car over the past century has exposed independence as yet another false god of the American experience.

Again, we should not be surprised by this outcome, because independence is not held in high regard within the biblical witness. The popular proverb "God helps those who help themselves" is an American invention and is nowhere to be found from Genesis to Revelation. A more biblical value that may be at the heart of our striving for independence is interdependence. Interdependence strives to empower the individual toward some productive end but allows individuals to achieve their maximum potential only in community.

25

Such interdependence is affirmed very early in the biblical witness when God declares that, "it is not good for . . . man to be alone" and makes for the first human a helpmate and a partner.[7] It is underscored in the teamwork of Moses and Aaron and in Jethro's advice for Moses to appoint judges to adjudicate cases among the people.[8] This notion of interdependence is probably best expressed in Paul's image of the fellowship in the body of Christ:

> Indeed, the body does not consist of one member but of many. If the foot would say, "Because I am not a hand, I do not belong to the body," that would not make it any less a part of the body. And if the ear would say, "Because I am not an eye, I do not belong to the body," that would not make it any less a part of the body. If the whole body were an eye, where would the hearing be? If the whole body were hearing, where would the sense of smell be? But as it is, God arranged the members in the body, each one of them, as he chose. If all were a single member, where would the body be? As it is, there are many members, yet one body. The eye cannot say to the hand, "I have no need of you," nor again the head to the feet, "I have no need of you." On the contrary, the members of the body that seem to be weaker are indispensable, and those members of the body that we think less honorable we clothe with greater honor, and our less respectable members are treated with greater respect; whereas our more respectable members do not need this. But God has so arranged the body, giving the greater honor to the inferior member, that there may be no dissension within the body, but the members may have the same care for one another. If one member suffers, all suffer together with it; if one member is honored, all rejoice together with it.[9]

The advantage that cities and traditional neighborhoods have over sprawling suburbs with respect to interdependence is that they allow people of a greater variety of ages to participate meaningfully in the culture. Young people, by being able to walk places and conduct transactions, are learning the rules and values of the adults in the community with whom they interact on their way. And elderly persons can be more visible and present (even if mostly sedentary) to pass on their wisdom and perspective to the younger generations.

Consider architect Christopher Alexander's advice on recognizing interdependence in community life:

> Persons at each stage of life have something irreplaceable to give and to take from the community, and it is just these transactions which help a person to solve the problems that beset each stage. . . . Patterns of mutual regulation occur between the very old and the very young; between adolescents and young adults, children and infants and these patterns must be made viable by prevailing social institutions and those parts of the environment

26

which help to maintain them—the schools, nurseries, homes, cafés, bedrooms, sports fields, workshops, studios, gardens, graveyards.[10]

If the church wants to be the "body of Christ" by including every member in its life, shouldn't the church advocate a communal life that can fully include all members of the society as well?

Freedom

A third and final false god that we have been tempted to worship in this country has been the god of freedom. Freedom has been narrowly understood as escape from external enemies or constraints. Many of our ancestors came to this country for the purpose of escaping persecution or the stifling class system of the Old World. And then, in time, as the East became more crowded and confining, once again they escaped to the frontiers of the West. But even that vast frontier could not provide an escape valve indefinitely. In 1893 Frederick Jackson Turner officially declared the American frontier closed. Around the same time, Henry Ford was tinkering with a mass production technique for the automobile.[11] The increasingly easy availability of automobiles during the first half of the twentieth century opened up one last frontier for this country and permanently changed the physical shape of our communities. The car has allowed us to escape by pushing our housing, shopping, and recreation to the very fringes of our population cores.

And thus was set in place a pattern of perpetual escape that we are still trying to make work today. As James Howard Kunstler puts it, "Americans, given the choice between civilizing their cities through public works, and using the car to escape the demands of civility, chose the car."[12] The problem with escapism as a way to deal with problems, as we have observed, is that it cannot go on forever. This is painfully obvious to anyone who has bought a suburban house on the very edge of town only to find a year or so later another development going up where there once was green space. Not only does this kind of development prove personally disappointing, it also builds resentment among people toward their neighbors for destroying their dreams.

The other problem with freedom as escape is that, again, it is not a necessarily Christian value and it is not in our best interest. There are great escape scenes within the biblical witness. The Israelites were able to escape from their slavery in Egypt through the mighty acts of their God.[13] Daniel and his friends were able to escape the lions' den.[14] Peter and Paul escaped imprisonment. And Paul used his authority with Philemon to urge him to allow Onesimus to escape his role as a slave.[15]

27

But freedom as we have understood it in this country is not exactly like the biblical accounts of escape. We tend to think of freedom as escape from anything or anyone that is annoying or inconvenient to us. Because of this potential confusion over the concept of escape in our culture, a better word to clarify the biblical understanding of freedom would be *liberation*. To be liberated means to be set free from oppression, and it can also mean to be set free to fulfill the role that God has set forth for a person. Liberation in the biblical witness also allows us to acknowledge the fact that often what we need liberation from is not an external enemy or an outside force but rather ourselves. We are "slaves of sin," according to Paul, and no matter how far out of town we drive to our home, that enslavement will persist.[16]

If we are inconvenienced or annoyed by living, working, and playing in the company of our fellow human beings, perhaps we need liberation from our selfishness and our willfulness rather than a massive home on a two-acre lot (soon to be surrounded by other massive homes on two-acre lots). Living in closer proximity to our neighbors forces us to make compromises of our needs and wants—sometimes allowing us to learn the difference between the two. And as we navigate the delicate balance between our needs and those of our neighbors, we are presented with opportunities to take social risks and talk to our neighbors as we come up with mutually acceptable solutions. When we successfully negotiate these informal social contracts, what we gain—in addition to a satisfying solution—is a deeper and more honest relationship with those among whom we live. When distance and avoidance constitute our sole strategy for coping with our neighbors, this kind of character and relational formation never happens.

We once hosted a play group at our house for the children of some of our friends. One of the participants was a two-year-old boy who lives in a house on a five-acre lot. During the course of the activities, his mother asked us how we could stand to live so close to our neighbors. We tried to explain that having neighbors close by takes a little more work, but it also allows for the kind of human community that we have come to appreciate. This point was completely lost on our guest. Interestingly enough, this woman's son was having a hard time sharing toys at play group on this particular day. Now this is typical behavior for a two-year-old, and we had all seen our own children exhibit similar behavior. However, by choosing to live in a setting where the adults would not have to share with their neighbors, this woman was limiting her ability to model healthy sharing for her son. In their particular environment, it would be easier to teach freedom as escapism rather than as true liberation.

28

■ Subsidizing Sprawl

In spending a great deal of time trying to convince people of the values of urban living and the peril of our suburban mentality, I have come to expect a certain resistance to this type of thinking. It is not that people will disagree with the content of what I am saying (although some people do just that). I may make some headway in encouraging people to choose individual identity over individualism, interdependence over independence, and liberation over escapism, and yet there is still some resistance. What they resist is not the values themselves but rather the antipopulist sentiment that seems to be implied in this perspective. Americans, as a whole, have a deep reverence for the free market and a deep skepticism for anything that seems to smack of elitism or authoritarianism. The free market—more so than our electoral system—has come to represent in our minds the will of the people. And it seems, at first glance, that people have freely chosen sprawl and all of its trappings with their hard-earned dollars. To suggest that we "should" do otherwise is perceived as an example of un-American social engineering.

For this reason it is important to understand the various forces behind our sprawl dilemma—specifically, those forces that do not represent free-market capitalism. The fact of the matter is that our government has played a much larger role in our current situation than individual consumers ever have.

Roads

A striking example of this is how the government poured public money into highway development and allowed an extensive and efficient streetcar system to go bankrupt. The Federal Highway Act of 1938 provided the funding for an ambitious interstate highway system. By 1953, the government had put almost $1 billion into 6,000 miles of interstate highway construction. President Eisenhower upped the stakes significantly when he signed into law the Federal-Aid Highway Act of 1952, which set into motion a twenty-year plan to build 41,000 miles of highways and began the unchallengeable practice of including billions of dollars each year in our federal budget for building roads.[17] In the year 1999 alone, the federal government contributed more than $83 billion toward highway construction.[18]

At the same time, public transportation was given almost no support from government funds. As Kenneth T. Jackson notes:

Unlike the road, which was defined as a public good and thus worthy of public support, mass transit was defined as a private business unworthy of aid. . . . Thus, Americans taxed and harassed public transportation even while subsidizing the automobile like a pampered child.[19]

Even today we see city after city embroiled in endless debate over the wisdom of putting a fraction of what is spent on roads toward the development of an adequate public transportation system. While our government was sparing no expense to encourage sprawl-type development, automobile manufacturers were demonstrating that they too were eager to contribute to the cause. General Motors went so far as to buy up struggling streetcar companies and close them down. GM was convicted of criminal conspiracy for this activity in 1950 (and was fined a mere $5,000), but the damage was already done.[20]

After a half-century of neglect and targeted attack, the quality and availability of public transportation was deteriorating, thus making the car more attractive by contrast. At the same time, new roads were being built, which made the car more convenient. Not only did the highways make it cost-effective to live farther and farther out of town, but also many of them cut right through the middle of the city—literally cutting the life force out of vital neighborhoods.

Housing

The second government policy favoring suburbanization was the effort to provide better housing for average citizens. The primary policy designed to meet this objective was the National Housing Act, passed in 1934.[21] This act provided guarantees on loans for qualified persons and required banks to make loans more affordable by lowering down-payment requirements and extending loan periods. This was a wildly successful government program, and it helped increase homeownership significantly during the years it was in effect. However, the Federal Housing Authority (FHA), created by the act, made policies that favored new homes in new neighborhoods over older homes in older neighborhoods. Not only did this fan the flame for suburban sprawl, but it also caused many people who had been living in the city to move out to the suburbs in order to get a loan. In addition to the direct effects of the FHA strategy, private banks began to adopt FHA policies in their general lending policies.

At the same time, the government was enacting legislation that would destroy many neighborhoods within historic cities. In 1949 Congress began to provide federal loans for cities to "redevelop" blighted urban areas. According to *National Geographic*, this "'urban renewal' raze[d] not only slums, but also stable low-income ethnic and African American neighborhoods."[22] This government policy had three major problems. First, enforcement was left to the local level, and very little of the public housing that was constructed was built in the newer suburban areas. Second, there was a requirement that dilapidated buildings be torn down in order for localities to receive the funds for new public housing. What the government didn't realize was that these dilapidated buildings, as chaotic as they looked from the outside, really helped to sustain the delicate texture of neighborhoods that were functioning adequately for the communities that lived there.

Last, the public housing structures that were built to replace the old buildings were so oppressive and destructive to community that they became far more dangerous and blighted places than anyone had imagined possible. The "projects," as they came to be known, separated businesses from residential areas, concentrated all of the residents into a few high-rise buildings, and left too much open space between buildings. It became all but impossible for shop owners and residents to monitor common areas, leaving large territories of their neighborhoods vulnerable to gangs and undesirable activities. Those who had no other options were confined to living their lives in fear, and everyone else fled to the suburbs as quickly as they could.

In sum, for the past half-century, government policy has strongly favored suburban housing over housing in historic cities and neighborhoods. And government policy has turned many of our best urban spaces into civic wastelands. This has greatly reduced the quality and availability of good urban housing for those who might prefer such a setting and has created a situation where the suburban option has become the only reasonable choice for many people. We must own up to the fact that it has not been solely the free market that has driven us to our current sprawl development patterns.

Zoning

The process of zoning for different uses also changed many of the organic patterns of neighborhood development. Originally, zoning was a tool to keep incompatible uses away from each other. As a policy tool it was developed to stabilize real estate values by preventing, for example, a tannery from opening next door to a home. But over time, zoning as a standard practice took on a life of its own and no longer was used merely as a tool to regulate extreme situations. In effect, zoning laws took civic planning out of the public domain and put it into the hands of bureaucrats and engineers who were more interested in neat and clean drawings and rules than in how things actually functioned in real life. The other use of zoning was for wealthy citizens to exclude undesirable residents from their neighborhoods. In 1926 the Supreme Court declared it legal for local governments to pass zoning laws that separated even compatible uses from each other.[23]

Zoning laws restricting multifamily structures (such as apartment buildings) from being built in the same area as single-family homes became commonplace. There was no compelling reason for this application of zoning laws other than to keep less wealthy people out of wealthy neighborhoods. Other questionable zoning practices began to emerge at this time and were similarly going unchallenged. Soon it became commonplace to exclude all commercial activity from residential areas. Thus, the practice of extreme separation was put into place, making it illegal in some places to have a corner grocery or coffee shop in a residential neighborhood and sometimes making sure that only houses of a similar size existed in the same area.

■ Illegal Neighborhoods

One convenient example of the impotence of the free market in our housing divisions is my own neighborhood. I live in a traditional neighborhood that is about a ten-minute walk from downtown. Because of its charm and proximity to the amenities of the city, it is a very popular neighborhood. You rarely will see a "For Sale" sign in this neighborhood, because houses routinely sell the day they go on the market. Houses on my street have continued to grow in value, regardless of the fluctuations of the real estate market, and have outpaced the market year after year.

One would think that the market would respond to this popularity by building similar types of neighborhoods in other parts of the city. But developers don't do this, because 60 percent of my neighborhood is noncompliant with the current zoning codes. We have a grocery store, a coffee shop, a bakery, and a hair stylist all within walking distance. Houses are "insufficiently" set back from the street. Most streets have alleys along the backs of the houses. And we have large mansions next door to small houses and even apartment buildings. My neighborhood serves as a constant reminder of the fact that the "invisible hand" of free-market capitalism is not solely responsible for our sprawling housing patterns of the last half-century. The reasons for our current situation are many and complex, and whether we like it or not, the way out will require more than just individual consumer choices.

Americans pride themselves on their ability to change and to adjust to new situations. And in this sprawl dilemma we see many people seeking out a more sustainable and satisfying solution. People are showing a willingness to give up some of their independence, individualism, and escapist tendencies to experience true community. But we need to change institutionally and structurally as we are changing individually if we truly wish to resist these false gods that have held us captive for so long.

From the Garden to Jerusalem

He drove out the man; and at the east of the garden of Eden he placed the cherubim, and a sword flaming and turning to guard the way to the tree of life.

Genesis 3:24

The idea of a modest dwelling all our own, isolated from the problems of other people, has been our reigning metaphor of the good life for a long time. It must now be seen for what it really is: an antisocial view of existence. I don't believe that we can afford to keep pretending that life is a never-ending episode of *Little House on the Prairie.* We are going to have to develop a different notion of the good life and create a physical form that accommodates it.

James Howard Kunstler, *Home from Nowhere*

 Annexing Eden

Missoula is the kind of place that prides itself on accepting differences of opinion on all sorts of matters. People tend to respect other people's right to think for themselves. And if they disagree on a particular issue, they generally are civil about it. This civility applies unless the issue happens to be annexation. Annexation is the process of incorporating terri-

34

tory into an existing political unit, such as a country, state, county, or city.[1] When a city annexes an adjacent neighborhood, the neighborhood becomes liable for city taxes, and it receives city services such as sewers and snow removal. Over the past decade or so, Missoula has annexed a number of areas.

As one might imagine, annexation is not always a popular policy among those affected by it. And there is usually a great deal of public outcry whenever a new annexation is being undertaken. For at least one of our residents, the idea of being hooked up to the city's sewer provides a poignant image on which to focus his disaffection with being connected to the city against his will. He reveals his cosmic struggle against an evil public in an impassioned letter to the editor:

> Are you on the end of the poop tube? They're comin' to getcha! The city, that is, with its runaway annexation. The city is interested in money and power. It increases money by bringing more people into the city to pay taxes. It increases its power by using fines, permit processes and fees on top of the taxes already imposed to control the private landowner. Without private property rights upheld, we are back to the feudal system of England. . . . Is that what you want, more government, by the government, and of the government? These are your neighbors. This is your yard. This is your home. Don't sit still and let it happen.[2]

The city here is portrayed as some kind of alien force with malicious intent toward this innocent property owner and his family. As the letter continues, the writer tones down his rhetoric somewhat to provide a more reasoned political explanation for the phenomenon of annexation, with a gross oversimplification of the development of the democratic tradition. Finally, the discussion moves beyond power politics for an appeal to writer's basic civil rights. His battle against the evil city becomes the last line of defense for the integrity of the American way of life.

Nowhere does this writer mention that the city, besides being a malicious agent of coercive power, has some amenities to offer as well. He accuses the city of "bringing people in," as if it were forcing people to live in proximity to itself against their will. He doesn't happen to mention that the city provides an economic base for employment as well as cultural opportunities and consumer conveniences. Most likely, the writer works, plays, and shops within the city. And unless he was an original homesteader in this region, these amenities were available at the time he built or purchased his house. So, in actuality, his relationship with the city is much more involved than just his paying taxes for a sewer hookup. He has been enjoying the benefits of living near a city for who knows how long and only now is being asked to pay his share of the cost of an urban lifestyle.

But his skepticism and fear of the city override these kinds of considerations, and he can see the city only as an alien threat to his settled way of life. This perspective, which views the city and its effects in direct opposition to the natural and healthy habitat of the human family, is not extreme or even unusual, but rather represents a dominant trend in many people's way of thinking.

Behind this point of view lies an idealized picture of human community that finds its origin in the Garden of Eden. Eden, whether explicitly referenced or hovering in the background, often provides the model setting for home and family against which all other forms of human community are unfavorably compared. This point of view recognizes the tragic circumstances that got us removed from the garden and takes for granted that getting back to the garden is the implicit goal for all rational humans. For those who have achieved some success in approximating the experience of Eden for their family, the "poop tube" of annexation gets the chilly reception that our primeval ancestors should have given the crafty serpent.

And one can easily see how this point of view has become established. After all, in the Bible, life does begin in a garden. Adam and Eve are originally located in a place called Eden, and there is no mention of concrete sidewalks, streetlamps, or sewage lines. The basic economic and political unit is simply a husband and a wife in their natural environment. Needless to say, there is no city government or city hall, because there is no city. And clearly, we were removed from that idyllic setting because of a transgression against our Creator. It's no wonder that people influenced by the story of Eden have had a deep-seated desire to return to the garden. The question that we must address, however, is whether or not that is really an appropriate goal for Christians. Are we meant to return to the garden and re-create Eden, or are we now destined for the more communal life of the city?

■ Ambivalent Cities

Cities of Sin

Whatever our future prospects might be with respect to the garden, the idea of finding redemption in the city seems highly unlikely as the biblical narrative continues beyond Eden. If being removed from the garden was the outcome of humanity's first sin against God, building a city was the outcome of the second.

After Cain kills his brother Abel, the Lord intensifies the curse of the land with regard to Cain and condemns him to being a fugitive on the earth.[3] Cain interprets this punishment as a threat to his very life, as well as banishment from a relationship with God.[4] The Lord seeks to comfort Cain by providing a mark of protection that will warn off those who would seek to harm him. But Cain, apparently unsatisfied with this degree of protection, decides to take matters into his own hands.

He builds a city and names it after his son Enoch. Cain's impulse toward city life seems to come directly out of a broken relationship with the land, his family, and his God. The city functions as a surrogate for these primary relationships, providing an alternate form of protection and provision for the banished human. The city continues to serve this kind of function even today. People run away from their families and their God to the city and its comfortable anonymity.

The next biblical city of note is the city of Babel, founded by Nimrod—a mighty warrior.[5] The residents of this city decide to build themselves a tower that reaches the heavens.[6] They do this as a way to make a name for themselves and to prevent them from being scattered throughout the earth. The seduction here is not so much self-preservation as self-assertion. They wish to make a name for *themselves* rather than looking to God for their identity. If this isn't made explicit in their own pronouncements, God's activity in frustrating their plans bears witness to their evil intent.

And again, we find people coming to the city, even today, in order to make a name for themselves. People come to the city to make their fortunes. They come to the city to make it on the stage or screen. Or they come to the city to appropriate the latest fashions and trends. As Frank Sinatra sings in "New York, New York," "If I can make it there, I'll make it anywhere."

Later, we come to a third city of note, with the building of Ramses.[7] This city is built by the Israelites who are enslaved in Egypt under the pharaoh. The building of this city is motivated not by fear or ambition, but rather by coercive power. The Israelites do not want this city and will not notably benefit from its construction but are forced to build it against their will.

Ramses, then, represents the tragic city. And, again, we continue to see situations of oppression and heartbreak in our cities today. In our cities, we find people enslaved to drugs, forced to work in inhumane sweatshops, and trapped in dead-end situations. The city has become for many people a place of profound oppression.

From the picture of the city contained in these three vignettes, it's no wonder that people's first response to the city is often one of revulsion.

We see in the city fearful and disenfranchised people. We see people so full of themselves and their accomplishments that they have lost all sense of proportion or humility. And we see broken and trapped people throughout the city. Jacques Ellul understandably concludes: "The spiritual power of the city must therefore clash with the spirit of grace. Such is the central problem that the city represents for Israel."[8]

From what we have seen so far, who wouldn't want to get back to the garden, or at least some approximation of it, rather than risk our future and the future of our families in the godforsaken context of the city? But this part of the biblical narrative takes us only into the first two books of the Old Testament, and there is much more of the story to uncover.

Good Cities

As the biblical narrative continues, we begin to see more positive references to the city. In the book of Deuteronomy, Moses recounts to the people what they can expect as they enter into the Promised Land. He catalogs all of the assets to be found in this new land, including houses, cisterns, vineyards, and olive groves. Surprisingly, the city is included in his list of the assets: "When the Lord your God has brought you into the land that he swore to your ancestors, to Abraham, to Isaac, and to Jacob, to give you—a land with fine, large cities that you did not build . . ."[9]

We might suppose here that Moses is simply being pragmatic in his description of the assets awaiting them in the Promised Land. Cities do have an economic and political value, regardless of their spurious origins. However, when we come to the book of Leviticus, we find that cities have become an important boundary between what is considered clean and unclean in a religious sense. And it is not the case (as we might presume from the narrative so far) that cities represent the apex of uncleanliness for the Israelites. But rather, just the opposite, the unclean places are to be found outside of the city.

When a leprous disease, mildew, or fungus appears in a house, "the priest shall command that the stones in which the disease appears be taken out and thrown into an unclean place outside the city."[10] It is not that the diseased stones should be taken out of the city that is interesting here—that is only logical. But rather, the increasing frequency with which the phrases "unclean place" and "outside the city" are together grouped throughout Leviticus should be noted. Three times in the fourteenth chapter alone we witness these phrases so combined.

The purpose of maintaining a distinction between clean and unclean for the Israelites was to maintain a ceremonial relationship with their God. In Leviticus, the Lord tells Moses and Aaron, "Thus you shall keep the people of Israel separate from their uncleanness, so that they do not die in their uncleanness by defiling the tabernacle that is in their midst."[11]

What seems to have happened here, between Exodus and Deuteronomy, is somewhat of a reversal in the status of the city. The city originates in a context of humanity separated from God. But in time, the city becomes an appropriate place for the Israelites to commune with their God.

Another interesting development that elevates the status of cities is the introduction of the cities of refuge:

> When you cross the Jordan into the land of Canaan, then you shall select cities to be cities of refuge for you, so that a slayer who kills a person without intent may flee there. The cities shall be for you a refuge from the avenger, so that the slayer may not die until there is a trial before the congregation.[12]

The cities of refuge, then, offer some protection against undisciplined vigilante justice. And as such, they suggest the city as a place—to borrow Daniel Kemmis's phrase—capable of grace.

■ A Place for My Name

Even this elevation to respectability is not the last word with regard to the city in the Bible. We find, as the biblical story unfolds, the city becoming more than just an acceptable place to commune with God. Far beyond this, we discover one particular city emerging as the exclusive center for the worship of God and the focal point for the all of the redemptive hope for God's people. The establishment of Jerusalem becomes a decisive turning point in the biblical portrayal of the city. It is to this significant story that we now turn.

David had defeated Saul and had taken his rightful position as king of Judah, with Hebron as his center of operation. Israel and Judah had formerly been at odds with each other, and the people of Israel were supposed to be loyal to Ishbaal. But they had become disillusioned with their king and could not see David as their enemy. David had won their hearts as a leader.

After Ishbaal is murdered, the Israelites turn to David and ask him to be king. The elders of Israel come to David and make their request, and they give three reasons why they feel he is the rightful king.[13] First, they claim David as their own flesh and blood. He is not an alien seizing power from strangers but is part of their community. His future is wrapped up in their future, because they are of one family. Second, they recognize David's military superiority. David, even under Saul, was a military hero, and under his leadership the Israelites felt that they would be safe from their enemies. They may also have felt that it was just to recognize David for his courage and valor. Last, they claim his divine right to be king. They recall his divine commission to be "shepherd" over the people of Israel. We see in this request by the elders of Israel three reasons why they looked to David to be the focus of their hopes and expectations for the future. David represented the unifying force of their covenant community. David represented the power and righteousness of the kingly office. And David represented the favor of the Lord, who had provided the definitive identity of the people of Israel.

David confirms the validity of their choice in his next move. Rather than sit back comfortably and enjoy the spoils of his newly gained power, he considers the well-being of this emerging nation as a whole. He decides to move his capital away from Hebron to avoid the appearance of favoring his own people. He chooses a city, in the territory of Benjamin, that had not been claimed by Israel or Judah. Jerusalem, currently occupied by the Jebusites, proves to be an ideal site for his new capital. The choice of Jerusalem is significant, because it represents a move away from petty tribalism to nation building on the part of Israel's new king. The city represents a developing political maturity for Israel and for her leaders.

And so in one last military victory, David easily conquers Jerusalem and makes it his new capital and the command post for his military operations. Jerusalem from this point on becomes known as the city of David. And when the king of Tyre recognizes his authority, David knows that "the LORD had established him as king over Israel, and that he had exalted his kingdom for the sake of his people Israel."[14]

David, unwilling to see his role as simply that of a political/military leader, now seeks to establish Jerusalem as a center of YHWH worship as well. He goes to Baalah of Judah and brings the ark of the covenant to Jerusalem with great celebration and solemnity. In this, David shows much more wisdom than his predecessor, Saul:

> Where Saul had neglected the Ark and driven its priesthood from him, David established both Ark and priesthood in the official national shrine. It was a masterstroke. It must have done more to bind the feelings of the tribes to Jerusalem than we can probably imagine.[15]

David is thus firmly established as the greatest of all Israel's kings. But in choosing Jerusalem as a focal point for his power, justice, and righteousness, he gives the Israelites a more durable place for their national hopes than simply in his charismatic personality. David's reign lasts about forty years, but the city of David endures considerably longer. Jerusalem, from this point on, is firmly fixed as the center of the hopes and fears of God's people and will continue in this role literally into eternity.

On one level, we see David's military, political, and even theological wisdom in the decision to choose Jerusalem as his capital. But long before David became king, we saw God himself laying the foundation for such a local presence among his people. In Deuteronomy, Moses gave the Israelites instructions for keeping the festivals. After outlining the details for the feasts and sacrifices, he indicated that they must keep these festivals at a place that the Lord would choose.[16] The specific location was not given at that point but would be disclosed at a later time.

Perhaps this is in David's mind when he expresses a desire to build a temple for God. But not even David can force God's hand in this way. God is going to choose the place for his people to gather and worship him, "I will provide a place for my people Israel and will plant them, so that they may live in their own place and be disturbed no more."[17]

In fact, David is not going to have the privilege of even seeing this place established in his lifetime. That honor will go to his son:

> When your days are fulfilled and you lie down with your ancestors, I will raise up your offspring after you, who shall come forth from your body, and I will establish his kingdom. He shall build a house for my Name.[18]

And as has been predicted, this "place" will be in the midst of a city:

> Since the day that I brought my people Israel out of Egypt, I have not chosen a city from any of the tribes of Israel in which to build a house, that my name might be there.[19]

Solomon does fulfill this prophecy by building a temple in Jerusalem. And the Lord confirms this activity by promising to put his name there forever.[20] This temple marks Jerusalem permanently as Israel's sacred space, where the Lord's people must go in order to commune with their God.

Even as Israel declines as a political/military force and the population becomes spread out farther and farther, Jerusalem remains the focal point in the Israelites' relationship with their God. The Psalms of Ascents, which were sung by the Jews on their way to Jerusalem for the feasts, are a good example of the connection that they continued to feel toward their city even if they did not personally reside there: "I was glad when they said to me, 'Let us go to the house of the LORD!' Our feet are standing within

41

your gates, O Jerusalem. . . . As the mountains surround Jerusalem, so the LORD surrounds his people."[21]

Isaiah, the most eloquent of the prophets, develops the evocative Zionist theology with its focus on Jerusalem. Over time, the word *Zion* becomes identified with the righteous reign of God and is inextricably connected with Jerusalem: "Look on Zion, the city of our appointed festivals! Your eyes will see Jerusalem, a quiet habitation, an immovable tent, whose stakes will never be pulled up, and none of whose ropes will be broken."[22]

What is interesting about Zionist theology is that it creates a language of hope that is centered on Jerusalem but is not directly tied to the current state of the city of Jerusalem and especially of its residents. For all of Isaiah's elevated praise for Jerusalem, he could also be her most severe critic: "How the faithful city has become a whore! She that was full of justice, righteousness lodged in her—but now murderers!"[23] It is as if Jerusalem is especially culpable for its shortcomings because it was so favored by God.

The holy city is thus firmly established in the minds of God's people as the context for their hope. The only question is whether Jerusalem will be able to live up to its name. This drama takes an interesting turn, however, with the coming of Jesus Christ.

■ Already and Not Yet

Jesus, in his birth, life, and death, transfers the local presence of God from the city of Jerusalem to himself. This is indicated at his birth, when the name Emanuel (God with us) is associated with him. And when Christ is being crucified, the curtain in the temple of Jerusalem is torn in two, indicating that God's presence is no longer going to be restricted to one location. Now God is accessible to everyone at any location through the mediating presence of the Holy Spirit.

One of the many implications of this radical shift of God's presence is that the city—even the holy city of Jerusalem—becomes much less significant as a physical context for our communion with God. That is why, when the temple at Jerusalem was destroyed in A.D. 70, Christians did not clamor to rebuild it. Nor did Christians initially feel compelled to replace Jerusalem with a new specific location for God's presence in one of their new centers of worship, such as Antioch or Rome.[24]

However, the reduced importance of the city is only one of the implications of the cross. Christ there defeated all of the enemies of humanity (sin, death, and the devil). But we don't immediately feel the full effect of his achievement. We have to wait until the consummation for the complete manifestation of Christ's victory. Only when Christ returns will we experience complete liberation from sin, death, and the devil and be reunited with our Lord to live and reign with him in eternity. In the meantime, we experience what theologians have called a situation of "already and not yet." By this they mean that we get a foretaste of our new existence as God breaks into our world, but we still have to wait for its fullness or perfection. We are profoundly shaped by the glorious vision of the future given to us, but we do not live as if it is already here.

John gives us the clearest expression of this redeemed existence in the Book of Revelation. It is notable in his book that the image John uses to describe his vision is not a return to the garden; nor is it some entirely new form of social relationship. Rather, we see the somewhat surprising return to the age-old concept of the city: "And I saw the holy city, the new Jerusalem coming down out of heaven from God, prepared as a bride adorned for her husband."[25]

So even though the city as an exclusive place of communion with God recedes from the time of Christ to the present, we find that it comes back again in the consummation. Once again we see the holy city Jerusalem as a place for God's name to dwell with his people.

As Christians, we are familiar with the idea that "our citizenship is in heaven."[26] We have understood this to mean that our allegiance to this world is tempered by the fact that there is another place called heaven, which will provide the setting for our eternal existence. Taking the model of New Jerusalem seriously means that we have to also take seriously the idea that in heaven we will be "citi-zens," or denizens of the city.[27] Whatever else that might mean, it at least means that to be a Christian means to be a city person. We may like or dislike particular cities, but we cannot despise the city itself.

We can be faithful to our calling to be city people in either an urban or a rural context. By their love for the holy city of Jerusalem, the Jews of Israel showed themselves to be a city people at heart. But only a certain percentage of Jews actually lived in the city of Jerusalem. There were a great many rural Jews who came to Jerusalem only for the great festivals of the year. In our contemporary context, we have similar possibilities. An urban dweller supports the city by direct participation in its life and its rhythms. And a rural dweller supports the city by enjoying the culture that is produced in the city, by providing food and other resources for the city, and by being a careful steward of the wilderness that surrounds the city. What is most problematic with regard to the city is suburbanization, which can drain the life out of the vital center of the city and doesn't support the city with any rural amenities. The suburban model seems destined for failure, because it does not take seriously the redemptive possibilities within the city.

■ Redemption, Not Return

If history shows the suburban development trends of the twentieth century to have been deeply flawed because of their basis in a deep misunderstanding of the city, at least it will have been a forgivable mistake. It is easy to miss the redemptive possibilities of the city because cities developed from spurious origins and have had some very real shortcomings throughout history. It is not the sin of the city that requires explanation, but rather its redemption. This radical change in the status of the city from a place of sin and unfaithfulness to the ultimate context for our redemption raises at least one important question: What can account for such a radical shift? Why did God take what looks to be one of humanity's worst inventions and use it as the primary context for our redemption?

The answer to this question is to be found in the question itself. Our God is fundamentally a God of *redemption*. God takes us (and our decisions) seriously. When we make mistakes—even profound ones—God does not obliterate the scars these mistakes leave on our character and start over. Rather, God takes our mistakes and reworks them into his divine plan and transforms our scars into something beautiful. Joseph said to his brothers when they repented of selling him into slavery, "Even though you intended to do harm to me, God intended it for good."[28] So also it seems that God has said of our cities, "You meant them to be a form of escape from me, I used them to draw you back to me."

And we see hints of this redemption theme all around the cities of the Bible. Cain's desire to flee to Enoch after killing his brother later finds a redeemed expression in the cities of refuge. The fear of the residents of Babel that they might be scattered is redeemed when the Israelites find cities in the Promised Land in which they can gather. The Hebrews longed to be free from their tyrant, Pharaoh, and eventually found a good king in the city of David. And finally, the Babel residents' desire to make a name for themselves is met in Jerusalem, where God has caused his name to dwell.

Redemption shows that God's power to redeem and restore is stronger than our ability to alienate and break down. But redemption is not always the strategy that we would choose if it were up to us. Often what we seek is a return to innocence. We want to forget about the past and start over. Psychologically, we repress painful memories. Relationally, we cut ourselves off from people who remind us of our past. And culturally, we ignore our history in favor of what is new and current.

Even in our cities our tendency is to wipe the slate clean and start over again, as the urban renewal and FHA housing programs tried to do. Or as private citizens, we prefer to act as if the city doesn't exist and to escape to our Edenic suburbs. We resent the city when it reminds us of our inextricable connection with the rest of sinful humanity by engaging in such policies as annexation. But for those who seek to take the Bible seriously, this cannot be our strategy. We cannot hate the city when our God is using it for good. We can support the city from a truly rural setting, but we cannot retreat to our own private gardens. That way has been closed off. We must at some level learn to take our cities seriously. Whether we live, work, worship, and play in our imperfect cities, or even just cheer for them at a distance, we need to look to our cities if we hope to catch a glimpse of what God has in store for us.

3

Waiting for Jerusalem

For here we have no lasting city, but we are looking for the city that is to come.

Hebrews 13:14

A city is a human artifact which is a collection of places and things. It is what we are born into and what we leave behind. What we hold in common is not only that which we share with the living, but that which we share with those before us and those after us. The city is therefore based on permanency.

Elizabeth Moule and Stefanos Polyzoides, in *The New Urbanism*

■ Claiming Our Cities for Christ

In the ministerial association meetings that I attend, there is frequent mention of "claiming our city for Christ." This usually gains a consensus and generates a high degree of enthusiasm among the various members of this group. But I am often left wondering what, specifically, is meant by such language. On the one hand, it evokes an image that I like very much—Christ in charge within the context of a redeemed city. This is none other than the New Jerusalem in which John has rooted all of our hope for redemption.

But John speaks of a time that has not yet arrived, and we read of it as a people who are between the cross and the consummation, in a time that has been best described theologically as "already and not yet." So the question that we must ask ourselves before we can appropriate such evocative language for our own context is whether using such language is, in fact, warranted. The way that many in the ministerial association seem to understand the concept of claiming our city for Christ involves sanctifying the geographical area of the city through the activities of personal evangelism and spiritual warfare.

We once viewed a film that documented a number of cities throughout the world that had been claimed for Christ in the sense that this phrase was being used in the group. In each of these cities, efforts of evangelism had been effective to the point that a significant portion of the population had made a personal decision to accept Christ as Lord. There were also many examples of certain people or places considered to be "strongholds for Satan" that were divested of their power through concentrated prayer. This change in the hearts of many individuals as well as in pockets of resistance brought a number of other benefits. In many cases, the jails, which had once been overcrowded, were now shown to be empty. In one city, gang activity and drug trafficking had been greatly reduced. In another area, the farmers were reporting record crops as the result of their prayers. And in all cases, the churches in the community were experiencing record growth.

The approach to the city and its prospects portrayed in this film has some merit. Certainly, there have been great revivals within cities throughout the history of the church. And if the cities shown in the film were truly experiencing genuine revivals, who could question the filmmakers' intention to note and celebrate places where individuals are placing their trust in Christ as Lord in record numbers? Such efforts could serve as a powerful witness to God's mercy and power. It seems fitting to use dramatic language like "claimed by Christ" to describe regions that are experiencing dramatic manifestations of God's Spirit.

However, the idea of a whole city or geographical region being "claimed for Christ" does present some problems. One problem with this approach is that claiming particular locations or regions for Christ doesn't seem consistent with the rest of the New Testament. It hearkens back to some old-covenant ideas where God focused his activity on specific locations and a particular people. We see some examples in the Old Testament of particular cities or sacred sites experiencing blessings because they removed the idols in the high places or because they housed the ark of the covenant. But in the New Testament, with the coming of Christ and the giving of his Spirit, this kind of geographical particularity seems to have come to an end. Nowhere does Paul imply that any of the cities in which he started churches have been "claimed for Christ," even though he considered his work in some of these places to be finished.[1] Paul was aware that

47

Christ won a decisive victory on the cross, and nowhere seems to imply that we need to improve the effectiveness of his victory by claiming things.

The second problem with this approach is that while it employs the term *city,* it doesn't take the specific form of the city seriously enough. It really seems to make no difference whether it is a city that is claimed for Christ or any other concentrated area of human activity. The Toronto Airport is understood to have been "claimed for Christ" by those who use such language, and there are myriad other examples one could cite. This approach speaks about Christ's influence on a geographic region, but the real impact is on the individuals within that region. The city itself does not necessarily experience any notable change as a result of this accelerated experience with Christ. We rejoice with the angels for each individual who decides to entrust his or her life to Christ, but this language of cities "claimed for Christ" really brings us no closer to an understanding of the redemptive possibilities of our cities.

The fact of the matter is that the only city in which we will see the full impact of being claimed for Christ is the New Jerusalem, which will descend when creation is restored at the consummation. Until that time, we will have to be content with imperfect prototypes of this glorious existence in places with names like Corinth and Philippi, Rome and Antioch, London and Paris, Nairobi and Sao Paulo, Seattle and even Missoula. In none of these places will we experience the overpowering impact of Christ's unmediated presence as the creatures do in John's vision. But in each of these places we can expect to see some unique foretaste of the redeemed existence as a result of their analogous relationship of form with the New Jerusalem. In that sense it may be appropriate to envision a city claimed by Christ to help us focus our efforts within the city. For the purpose of identifying redemptive possibilities in our provisional cities, we can ask ourselves the question, What would a redeemed city look like?

I once encouraged an adult Sunday school class at our church to picture Missoula (our provisional city) claimed by Christ insofar as it was possible for us to imagine it. After setting aside the question of exactly what percentage of the population would have to be Christian for Missoula to deserve such distinction, we began to picture it in our minds. To help the class organize their thoughts, I gave them a series of questions to consider. The questions ranged from the individualistic and behavioral to the social and institutional and, finally, to the physical and cultural:

- Would we notice a difference in how people treated one another when they passed on the street?
- Would people be more joyful in their demeanor?
- Would there be different traffic patterns on Sunday?

- Would bars, strip clubs, and casinos see a change in business?
- Would there be less litter in the streets?
- Would there be the need for jails?
- Would there be less work for police officers?
- Would there be a need for lawyers?
- Would there be more or fewer food banks?
- Would there be an increase or decrease in social services?
- If there were savings from reduced police and social services, would the savings go toward more parks or greater tax breaks?
- Would there be a flourishing or a diminishing of the arts?
- Would people spend more or less time at work?
- Would voter turnout be increased or decreased?
- Would houses tend to be closer together or farther apart?
- Would our public buildings (courthouse, library, and post office) be more grand or more plain?
- Would there be public celebrations of Christian holidays?

It was fascinating to observe how unanimous the response was to certain questions and how divided we became over others. A few left us in absolute confusion. Of course, this exercise was almost pure speculation, and no one assumed that we were creating an accurate picture of the New Jerusalem. However, it also became clear that how we answered these questions revealed some of our basic assumptions regarding salvation, redemption, and the nature of God.

It should not have been surprising that our Sunday school class encountered some division as they tried to sort out some of these questions. Over the past century, an analogous division among Christians in this country has been taking shape. This division has not emerged out of a different approach to picturing redemption in any kind of explicit way, but rather can be seen in how two groups of Christians have divided over the issue of how to do ministry in the city. These two groups have been variously labeled, but for our purposes I will call them private Christians and public Christians.[2]

■ Private Christians

The first group that we will be looking at is the private (also known as evangelical) Christians. The ministerial group to which I referred at the beginning of this chapter best fits into this category. Private Christians understand Matthew 28:19–20 as the basic mandate for the Christian church:

> Go therefore and make disciples of all nations, baptizing them in the name of the Father and of the Son and of the Holy Spirit, and teaching them to obey everything that I have commanded you. And remember, I am with you always, to the end of the age.

To this end, private Christians focus the majority of their efforts on evangelism and personal holiness. They may take part in other kinds of activities, such as feeding the hungry, but the evaluative criterion for these kinds of efforts is almost always the potential for evangelism and converting the individual. They may be concerned with societal issues like poverty and alcoholism, but their approach to solving these problems usually involves helping the individual to find victory over these maladies through his or her relationship with Christ.

In addition to this positive focus on evangelism and personal holiness, the strategy of private Christians with respect to the city has also been shaped throughout the twentieth century by a number of negative factors. The rapidly expanding cities of the industrial era brought to light rampant moral corruption among the masses who lived and played there. A theological response to these problems known as premillennialism began to take hold among certain members of the Christian community. Unlike postmillennialists, who thought that things were going to get better and better in preparation for Christ's return, premillennialists believed that things were going to get worse and worse until Christ returned to save us from ourselves.

Private Christians were profoundly shaped by this premillennialism, which provided a theological framework for their discomfort with the current state of affairs in the world. It became characteristic among this group of Christians to mistrust the "world" and to encourage separation from it:

> Once upon a time in the West, worldliness and separation were code words among gospel people. Worldliness meant smoking, drinking, ballroom dancing, novel reading, theater- and movie-going, makeup for women, deodorant for men, mixed bathing for adults, and late nights for children. Separation meant eschewing all of the above, being frugal at home, ignoring fashion, fleeing from luxury, being in church several times on Sunday, and building life around Bible study, personal evangelism, missionary support, and perhaps some local philanthropy. Most exponents of this form of pietism worked hard, looked after their families, and were warm-hearted and generous to those they helped, but their interests were narrow. As those in the world but not of it, they tried to have as little to do with it as

possible. They spoke of a coming apostasy and breakdown of community life, and watched fatalistically to see if it was happening.[3]

This divestment from the world and the surrounding culture was made especially manifest in the private Christians' reaction to the city, from which this doomed culture was emanating.

Another negative way that private Christians formed their approach to the city was in their growing suspicion of the theological convictions of their historic denominations. The Social Gospel movement was emerging as an alternative response to deplorable conditions in the expanding cities. At first the Social Gospel movement was characterized simply by its pragmatism. Its chief proponent, Walter Rauschenbusch, emphasized religious action on behalf of the poor as being indicative of the validity of a person's faith. He did not deny outright the importance of belief; he simply assigned it a lesser importance in the life of a Christian. Private Christians, however, took this as a dangerous development:

> The threat that conservative evangelicals perceived in the Social Gospel was not that it endorsed social concern—evangelicals themselves often made similar endorsements. It was rather that the Social Gospel emphasized social concern in an exclusivistic way which seemed to undercut the relevance of the message of eternal salvation through trust in Christ's atoning work.[4]

Over time this suspicion grew deeper, as the Social Gospel took hold within the historic denominations. The Social Gospel became associated with all sorts of theological positions that made private Christians uncomfortable. One result of this suspicion was a movement away from the historic denominations through the creation of nondenominational Bible schools, parachurch ministries (Young Life, Campus Crusade for Christ, Youth for Christ), and independent mission agencies. And even within the denominations there emerged evangelical subgroups that were critical of the denominations as a whole. For a Christian to show any interest in social concern immediately raised suspicions among the private Christians.

Last, private Christians established an aspect of their identity by pulling out of the institutions of mainstream culture. This development was brought to a head by the well-publicized Scopes trial of 1925. The case itself was not nearly as spectacular as the coverage of it in the media. It was presented by the media as a battle between conservative Christian creationists and rational moderates. As George Marsden observes:

The central theme was, inescapably, the clash of two worlds, the rural and the urban. In the popular imagination, there were on the one side the small town, the backwoods, half-educated yokels, obscurantism, crackpot hawkers of religion, fundamentalism, the South, and the personification of the agrarian myth himself, William Jennings Bryan. Opposed to these were the city, the clique of New York—Chicago lawyers, intellectuals, journalists, wits, sophisticates, modernists, and the cynical agnostic Clarence Darrow.[5]

Technically, the creationists won the battle: John Scopes was prohibited from teaching evolution. But in the mind of mainstream America, the moderates had won the war. Conservative Christians, from this point on, were seen as ridiculous figures and were pushed to the margins of the culture. As Marsden further observes, "in the trial by public opinion and the press, it was clear that the twentieth century, the cities and the universities had won a resounding victory, and that the country, the South, and the fundamentalists were guilty as charged."[6]

By the middle of the twentieth century, then, the identity of the private (or evangelical) Christian was formed. He or she was focused on evangelism and personal holiness. He or she sought to maintain holiness not in the midst of the world, but rather by withdrawing from the world. Whether they were affiliated with a historic denomination or not, the private Christians tended to be suspicious of the denominational leadership and did not look to these leaders for their theological moorings. And they gave up on attempts to have a voice in cultural institutions, such as the political realm, the media, and the universities. With respect to the cities, private Christians kept their distance. They continued to pray for and evangelize those in the cities, but they did not look to the city itself as a redeemable place.

Private Christians, despite this mainstream invisibility, thrived during the twentieth century. They were numerically strong and committed to the cause of the gospel. They even began to regain some of their political voice in the last two decades of the century. But as the twenty-first century begins, we see two persistent weaknesses in this group of Christians. The first has been that their experience of the gospel has been powerful but thin. They have focused on the issue of personal conversion to such an extent that they have an underdeveloped sense of the fullness of salvation. So much of their energy has been focused on battling against what they have understood to be activities of a worldly culture that they haven't noticed how the more subtle values of the culture has crept into their way of thinking.

In particular, they have picked up the individualism of our American culture and imported it directly into their churches and their theology.

David Wells powerfully documents this shift from biblical to cultural values:

> The biblical interest in righteousness is replaced by a search for happiness, holiness by wholeness, truth by feeling, ethics by feeling good about oneself. The world shrinks to the range of personal circumstances; the community of faith shrinks to the range of personal friends. The past recedes. The Church recedes. The world recedes. All that remains is the self.[7]

The second shortcoming of the private Christians has been the limited range of their impact upon the population. Despite strong numbers, the private Christian movement has been predominantly a white, middle-class phenomenon. Because private Christians have shied away from anything that might be considered to be social Christianity, they have not had a wide appeal among disenfranchised groups, such as ethnic minorities and the poor. This has been the case even when members of these groups have been more sympathetic with the theological convictions of the private Christians than with those of their mainstream counterparts.

■ Public Christians

If the private Christians emphasize the Great Commission of Matthew 28:19–20 in their calling, then the public Christians have taken Matthew 25:31–46 as the focus of their efforts:

> When the Son of Man comes in his glory, and all the angels with him, then he will sit on the throne of his glory. All the nations will be gathered before him, and he will separate people one from another as a shepherd separates the sheep from the goats, and he will put the sheep at his right hand and the goats at the left. Then the king will say to those at his right hand, "Come, you that are blessed by my Father, inherit the kingdom prepared for you from the foundation of the world; for I was hungry and you gave me food, I was thirsty and you gave me something to drink, I was a stranger and you welcomed me, I was naked and you gave me clothing, I was sick and you took care of me, I was in prison and you visited me." Then the righteous will answer him, "Lord, when was it that we saw you hungry and gave you food, or thirsty and gave you something to drink? And when was it that we saw you a stranger and welcomed you, or naked and gave you clothing? And when was it that we saw you sick or in prison and visited you?" And the king will answer them, "Truly I tell you, just as you did it to one of the least of these who are members of my family, you did it to me." Then he will say to those at his left hand, "You that are accursed, depart from me into the eternal fire prepared for the devil and his angels; for I was hungry

and you gave me no food, I was thirsty and you gave me nothing to drink, I was a stranger and you did not welcome me, naked and you did not give me clothing, sick and in prison and you did not visit me." Then they also will answer, "Lord, when was it that we saw you hungry or thirsty or a stranger or naked or sick or in prison, and did not take care of you?" Then he will answer them, "Truly I tell you, just as you did not do it to one of the least of these, you did not do it to me." And these will go away into eternal punishment, but the righteous into eternal life.

The public (or mainline) Christians in this country have understood their calling as a mandate to meet the physical needs of the poor. Whereas the private Christian dealt with the issue of poverty by encouraging individuals to get saved and then to let the Holy Spirit clean up their lives, public Christians have focused their efforts on the root causes of poverty and setting up institutions to provide for people in need.

However, like the private Christians, public Christians in the beginning of the twentieth century formed their identity and their approach to the city not only on the basis of what they were for, but also on the basis of what they were against. Specifically, they distinguished themselves from the evangelistic efforts of private Christians by focusing their efforts on the transformation of the world by creating institutions in the city. Their rallying cry became the "kingdom of God on earth."[8] And, as was mentioned above, being more concerned with pragmatic results than they were with precise doctrine, they found a weakening of their theological distinctions over time.

This top-down and theologically weak approach hurt the cause of public Christians in two ways. On the one hand, focused as they were on institutional forms of power, they began to lose credibility among the church membership that they were supposed to be representing. As Martin Marty relates:

One year I counted that the United Methodists had 63 resolutions on boycotting this wine and that . . . and boycotting lettuce and not buying Nestlé and all that. But I never met a Methodist who agreed with any of it. It's just what they passed at the summer convention.[9]

A second and related problem was that without strong theological moorings, the national leadership was often perceived as having a "radical agenda" that went beyond the theological moorings of the church at large. Without strong theological convictions to guide church policy, the denominational church leadership was vulnerable to taking its cues more from the intellectual culture as a whole than from any unique Christian perspective.

With regard to a strategy for the city, it became a tendency for the institutional leadership to articulate a vision for the city that did not necessarily represent the vision of the members of their churches or the people whom they were purporting to serve. While the institutions that they had formed continued to do a good job of feeding the hungry and providing various social services, their credibility as a distinctively Christian leadership was limited.

■ Populating Jerusalem and Forcing the Kingdom

When we consider this two-party division within American Christianity, we see the origins of two types of responses to the city within the Christian community. The private Christians either mistrust the city for its worldliness and its cultural power or they fail to see its relevance beyond their mandate for evangelism. The only positive way to characterize their relationship to the city is to say that they are focused exclusively on populating the New Jerusalem (that is to come) through their efforts of personal evangelism. By sharing the gospel with individuals and seeking their conversion to faith in Christ, they are increasing the numbers of those who will be included in the heavenly city when Christ returns.

With regard to the imagination exercise at the beginning of this chapter, private Christians would see a city claimed by Christ first and foremost as one where most or all of the population had accepted Jesus Christ as Lord and Savior. People would be kind to people on the street, and litter would be reduced, because each of these Christians would be seeking to live holy lives. There would be traffic jams on Sundays as people poured into churches. Bars and strip clubs would be devoid of patrons and would eventually shut down. Jails would be empty.

But there would be little consensus about what people would do when they weren't at church once the task of evangelism had been completed. There would be little agreement as to the increase or decrease in the arts, participation in voting, or what communal celebration would be like. This is because private Christians focus more on conversion than on the salvation of the world and more on avoiding impure behaviors than on engaging in redemptive behaviors.

The public Christians, on the other hand, have noticed and invested in their cities throughout the twentieth century. They have tried to be faithful to the gospel by attempting to make the values in their cities more in line with biblical values, as they understood them. Where public Christians have fallen short has been in overstepping their role with respect to the city. This language of "the kingdom of God on earth" too often has meant forcing their version of the kingdom on an unresponsive populace, claiming the power of a constituency that is not fully on board with their efforts.

In addition to these kinds of weaknesses, they have failed to acknowledge the limited role of kingdom building in the ultimate scope of things. And they have made issues of theological truth (and even a relationship with God) secondary to practical goals. They have rightly noted that the gospel has profound communal and social implications, but they have failed to recognize that the battle for the kingdom still takes place within each human heart. And they have failed to realize that it is the truth that will set people free.

Ultimately, their model cities, developed through practical goals, will not remain a vital part in the history of our salvation. Even a city full of justice and mercy will eventually be destroyed and replaced by the New Jerusalem. All that will be left will be relationships—relationships between individuals and Christ, relationships among believing brothers and sisters, and a restored relationship between Christians and the created order. Public Christians, in their efforts to force the kingdom, have neglected the essential mandate with respect to restored relationships.

When public Christians envision a city claimed by Christ, they might see institutions operating in a just manner. Wealth would be distributed evenly, and social services would be available to all. Communal celebrations might be advocated but might represent a particular ideological bent rather than resonate with the population as a whole. If my Presbyterian church calendar provides any clues, we could expect to see, on any given weekend, public events to "celebrate diversity," "rally against injustice," "respect the environment," or engage in "dialogue with other faiths." The question of whether this is what the citizens of the city actually wanted to focus on in a public event might never come up.

As we can see, both private and public Christians could benefit from taking the city more seriously as an independent entity in the history and future of their salvation. There is a naïveté in ignoring the city and trying to replace it with a sanitized and private world of Christian culture. And there is an arrogance in trying to shape cities into our institutional vision of what justice and righteousness should look like. A good place for both groups to start would be to simply recognize their cities and how God might already be using their cities for the purpose of redemption.

The fact that they haven't yet done so can be seen in that neither group would give much thought, in the opening exercise, to the physical features of the city. The density of houses or the grandeur of public buildings would most likely not be seen by either group as relevant to its redeemed character. I believe that this is because neither public nor private Christians really see their *cities* through the lens of their divergent Christian worldviews. The private Christians see the people in the city (or rather their souls), and the public Christians see abstract institutions. But neither group has really taken the physical form of their cities very seriously over the past century. To find a way past this oversight, we will begin by looking at two constructive models, from the areas of philosophy and politics, before we attempt a new Christian theology of the city.

■ Redemption in the City: A Philosophical and Political Perspective

Albert Borgmann and the Postmodern City

Albert Borgmann provides one example, from a philosophical perspective, of a constructive model for this kind of approach. In his book *Crossing the Postmodern Divide,* Borgmann asserts that the modern era is coming to an end. Modernism has not yet been replaced with a new era and, as a society, we are currently faced with two divergent courses that we might pursue. The first involves various forms of what he calls *hypermodernism,* which is a sort of desperate attempt to hold on to some of the features of the modernist project without the support of broad public consensus in its underlying assumptions. The hypermodernist strategy advocates a hyperactive pace of life combined with ongoing technological achievement, which are together supposed to solve all of our current problems and bring us a brighter future. These strategies are supposed to make our lives easier and more efficient, but they actually end up pulling us away from reality and making us anxious and lonely. An alternative response to the demise of the modern era is what he calls *postmodern realism.* Postmodern realism accepts the postmodern critique of modernism while avoiding many of the ambiguities so often associated with the term *postmodernism.* Postmodern realism involves three strategies that together offer a genuine alternative to the prevailing culture of hypermodernism. These strategies include what he calls focal realism, patient vigor, and communal celebration.

Focal realism is a meaningful encounter with an object or being that has an independent reality. It has to do with an interface between humanity and what Borgmann calls eloquent things. Engaging in a craft, riding a horse, hiking in the wilderness, and playing a violin are all examples of practices that involve focal realism. Putting a CD in your stereo or turning up your thermostat do not. Focal practices require the learning of a skill and an encounter with a real object. Focal realism can also include such daily activities as "athletics, the culture of the table, the culture of the word, and worship."[10]

As a correlated strategy, *patient vigor* comes from engaging in focal practices in the midst of the limits and contingencies that are placed upon people who live and work in the context of a community. As Borgmann notes, "being a moral virtue, patience, like its athletic sibling, is a habitual skill, acquired gradually and maintained through exercise."[11] As we pursue focal practices in the midst of our community, we learn a kind of patience that is vigorous and humane rather than sullen and isolating. The simple activity of gardening or learning to ride a bike among friends and neighbors or worshiping week by week in the midst of a busy and vibrant neighborhood can develop within us a kind of patient vigor that shapes our identity.

And last, Borgmann advocates *communal celebration*, which is just a rediscovery of focal practices and patient vigor among the community as a whole:

> Unless we are able to discover and nourish in the community and in the city those focal things and practices that are thriving in the family and in the country, the underlying reality of the postmodern era will languish everywhere. The symmetry that obtains in the small between a focal thing and a vigorous person joined in a focal practice needs to be discovered and recovered at large.[12]

Communal celebration happens when the members of a community (who have all been engaged in their own focal practices) gather to celebrate some shared aspect of their identity.

These three strategies, Borgmann suggests, can all be practiced within the context of a vibrant city. To demonstrate this, he suggests seeing the city through the framework of the traditional church calendar. Within the liturgical year there is both ferial (or common) time and festal (or celebratory) time.[13]

The daily city provides the context for ferial time in bringing into harmony human and natural rhythms of the day and of the year. This can be seen in a contrast between the ordinary city and the modernist achievement of the twenty-four-hour supermarket:

> Street life has its circadian and seasonal rhythms. The street wakes up in the morning with a spurt of busyness, relaxes in mid-morning, gathers

momentum toward noon, calms down once more in the afternoon, becomes roily between the end of work and dinner, and settles into a steady pace of activities in the evening. Street life tends to be lazier in the summer, bracing in the fall, restrained in the winter, and exuberant in the spring. In a well-lit, air-conditioned, twenty-four-hour supermarket, however, time decays to a featureless flow that feebly reflects the changes of the real world outside.[14]

Even such simple activities as getting to work, having lunch, and shopping can be occasions for focal practices when we live in a city that is mixed in use and pedestrian in scale.

This distinction can also be seen as we consider festal (or celebratory) time. While modern culture has tried to commodify celebration by making it something that we could purchase and enjoy in the privacy of our own homes, the city quite naturally provides the setting for true celebration. Genuine celebration, Borgmann insists, must include elements of reality, community, and divinity.[15] Borgmann sees true celebration in place in a minor league baseball game played in town, a powwow on the reservation, a choral festival, and (most importantly) in the celebration of the sacraments at our local churches. Celebration that is contrived (like high art) or overly commercialized (like professional baseball) falls short of the acts of informal and spontaneous celebration that take place throughout the ordinary city.

Daniel Kemmis and the Good City

Daniel Kemmis provides a political model for seeing redemptive possibilities in our cities. Kemmis, a former mayor of Missoula, has noted an increasing cynicism about political life in this country. Time and time again, the American public places its hopes and ideals in the national office of president of the United States, only to find its hopes disappointed. Kemmis has come to the conclusion that no solution will be found in a policy targeted at the national level, because the scale is too large. He calls us back to our local context, to our cities, and to basic traditions like the Missoula Farmers' Market as a place to find healing for our political condition:

Why would anyone even imagine that something like the Farmers' Market could play a role in mending a suffering democracy? Fixated as we are on "important" state and national issues such as term limits, campaign finance reform, crime, health care, and welfare reform, this suggestion seems at first to be merely frivolous.

59

But, in fact, none of the other paths to reform on which people expend so much energy will reverse the decline of democracy, and none of the policies that we enact to deal with pressing problems such as poverty, racism, environmental damage, and drug and alcohol abuse will do any more than slow the worsening of these evils until we begin to understand the political importance of events like the Farmers' Market. No amount of reforming institutions that are widely and rightly perceived to be beyond human scale will heal our political culture until we begin to pay attention once again to democracy as a human enterprise. Without healing the human base of politics, we will not restore democracy itself. One thing alone will give us the capacity to heal our politics and to confront the problems and opportunities that politics must address. That one thing is a deeply renewed human experience of citizenship.[16]

Kemmis sees the city and such elements as the Farmers' Market as laboratories for citizenship because they teach us to live near and with one another while maintaining a degree of civility. But what makes the Farmers' Market effective is more than just how it allows us to secure the bare commodities of life for ourselves without killing one another. The Farmers' Market brings us flowers, fresh coffee, and music along with our weekly supply of vegetables. And the Farmers' Market allows us to connect with our neighbors week by week as we shop with and amongst them. The Farmers' Market has political problems and issues. There is limited space for multiple vendors, and there are cultural differences between the Montana natives and the Hmong immigrants who jointly run the market. But these political issues are resolved among people who know one another's stories and live amongst one another. The politics of the Farmers' Market never loses its human scale, as politics almost always does at the national level.

At the core of our national political malaise, Kemmis finds, are the twin evils of abstraction and distraction. Abstraction has to do with when we "attempt to 'abstract' general principles from particular situations and then apply the abstracted principle to every particular situation."[17] He cites federal policies that are applied to localities like Missoula without consideration for local conditions or the will of local residents. Every misapplied law based on such abstraction tears at the political fabric and alienates us from political life.

Abstraction is what threatens politics at the national level; distraction is its local counterpart. Distraction involves activities that prevent us from engaging in our political or civic life. As Kemmis notes:

From drugs and alcohol to TV and workaholism, we are increasingly a society that fulfills T. S. Eliot's description of a people "distracted from distraction by distraction." There is hardly a public menace we can name that is not in some sense caused by one or another of the million ways in which our society teaches and enables us to abstract and distract ourselves—to escape in one way or another from the concrete presence of the here and now.[18]

An apt example of this kind of distraction is the all-too-common occurrence of the suburban commuter spending an hour in his or her private automobile, followed by another hour eating dinner in front of the TV, and then finally popping in a video before bed.

The city, of course, won't automatically heal these deep-seated traditions of abstraction and distraction that we have developed as a culture over the years. But the traditional city will provide many more opportunities for human contact and relationships than we will find in the suburbs. And these ordinary contacts and the relationships to which they can lead are the absolutely necessary building blocks for any kind of renewal in our political life.

Albert Borgmann and Daniel Kemmis, then, provide two models for actually seeing the elements of the city from two particular disciplines. Neither provides *the* model that ought to be adopted by the Christian community as it seeks to make sense of the city. But they both provide rich resources for recovering a vision for the city and for teaching us again about fundamental words like *celebration* and *citizenship* that would enrich any Christian's understanding of his or her city.

In particular, I think that both private Christians and public Christians could find help with their shortcomings from these two thinkers. Private Christians have a cultural problem. They have rejected the dominant culture out of a sense of fear but have not envisioned a replacement for the dominant culture out of their own communal life, because they have been focused more on the moment of conversion than on the fullness of salvation. In the absence of a coherent cultural vision, they have inadvertently appropriated more subtle elements of the dominant culture (such as individualism and consumerism) into their daily lives. Private Christians could learn from Borgmann about the reality, community, and divinity required for true celebration as they try to construct their own culture or contribute to the culture at large.

Public Christians, on the other hand, have a political problem. They have hitched their cart to the dominant cultural institutions and have lost some sense of their own distinctive identity as Christians. They have focused on the institutional elements of their churches and have lost touch with both the people in the churches and the people of the world whom they purport to serve. Public Christians could learn from Kemmis how to restore the human scale to the politics of the church. Church politics could lose some of its oppressive and irrelevant character if it were once again seen at a local level in a relational context. Church politics, like its secular counterpart, is really just an attempt to live and work together within our distinctive covenant identity.

The Christian community as a whole has a great deal to learn from people like Albert Borgmann and Daniel Kemmis when it comes to seeing our cities. But ultimately, we need to make sense of our cities from our distinct theological perspective. We have a rich theological heritage to draw from, but we need to apply it anew to the city that we have failed to see over the last century. A great constructive project awaits us. It is to a beginning of that project that we now turn.

4

Learning to See Our Cities: A Theological Approach

Walk about Zion, go all around it, count its towers, consider well its ramparts; go through its citadels, that you may tell the next generation that this is God, our God forever and ever. He will be our guide forever.

Psalm 48:12–14

Just as it is difficult to imagine the concept of family independent of the home, it is near-impossible to imagine community independent of the town square or the local pub.

Duany, Plater-Zyberk, and Speck, *Suburban Nation*

■ Losing Our Sight

A couple of years ago, I was in the market for a new bicycle. We had just moved to Missoula, which is relatively flat and compact, and a bicycle seemed to be the ideal way to get around. I hadn't really thought much about bicycles since asking for a new one for Christmas when I was ten, so I had a lot of catching up to do. As I tried to keep up with the merits of titanium frames and suspension systems that surpass that of my first car, I began to notice an interesting phenomenon around town. It seemed as if the number of bicycles in Missoula had increased exponentially since I had begun looking for one. Could it be that everyone was new to town and wanting a bicycle as I was? I soon figured out that the number of bicycles hadn't significantly changed in Missoula, but rather my shopping for a bicycle had raised my awareness of bicycles. The bicycles had always been there; it's just that I had begun to see them for the first time.

If our awareness of a particular phenomenon can be heightened by paying particular attention to it, a corresponding truth must surely be that our awareness of a phenomenon is lowered through our lack of attentiveness to it. I began to see bicycles again only because at some point I had ceased to see them. And certainly there must be other phenomena that we fail to see. It is my growing impression that in the decades following World War II we have ceased to see our cities and traditional neighborhoods in this country, because more and more of us have ceased to live, work, and play in these kinds of settings, choosing instead the suburban tract development and the "box" chain retail store to meet our residential and commercial needs.

I was at a conference last spring in which one of the participants had mentioned a book popular in Christian circles that includes a story of the author's personal decision to turn off the TV after dinner and instead walk around the block in her neighborhood with her son. This simple decision led to all kinds of interesting developments in their personal relationship and in their spiritual lives. After hearing this touching story, the thought struck me that this personal story was highly dependent on some increasingly rare features of our built environment.

I couldn't help but wonder if anyone in the room realized that out of the countless new-home developments thrown up in this country over the past year or so, few of them include a sidewalk to walk on, a block to walk around, or anything resembling what used to be understood as a neighborhood. Now, who's to say that if this author had taken her son on a walk down their cul-de-sac to the collector road, their experience would have been any less profound? I only know from personal experience that I can walk only so far in a tract development with five standard house designs, looking at an endless sea of garage doors, with no coffee shop, apartment building, or true park to break the monotony of the single-family detached house, before my TV is starting to look pretty interesting by comparison. But this is in fact the overwhelming style of the "neighborhoods" that are today being built.

We do not see cities or traditional neighborhoods in this country because we have not lived in them or thought specifically about them for a long time. We tend to think of cities as abstractions—a city is a place where humanity is gathered in large numbers. And so our discussions about the cities tend to be indistinguishable from discussions about crowds. What are the problems and pitfalls of humanity in its aggregate form? We've given very little thought to the physical structure of our cities and how that provides the framework for the human relationships that go on in these places. This intellectual oversight in our culture has led to bad policies, which in turn have made our cities harder to see. Consider the Federal Housing Administration's clear preference in their loan program for suburban-sprawl housing over urban neighborhoods and the ill-fated "urban renewal" program of the 1950s and 1960s, which destroyed the fabric of the urban core in favor of the inhumane, monolithic "projects." This oversight has been reflected in our theology as well. Try to find any concrete description of what actually constitutes a city in our myriad theologies of the city, and you will see what I mean. The time is ripe, therefore, for a theology of the city that takes into account its physical structure. This chapter is an attempt to provide some starting points for such a project.

■ Resurrection Cities and the Communal Context of Our Redemption

Let us begin with the notion of physicality itself and how it has dropped off of our radarscope of late. Consider the word *community,* for instance. *Community* used to mean almost exclusively those people who lived in proximity to us. Community couldn't easily be divorced from the idea of physical presence. We still find some examples of *community* being used in that sense, but in order to signify this use one needs to add some kind of a qualifier such as *intentional* to the word *community*. The far more common use of the word has to do with those who share certain interests. It is more common to hear of the gay community or the Christian community without any expectation that members of these "communities" live anywhere near one another. They aren't even expected to know one another.

We find this trend pushed to the extreme by our modern technology. The Internet has allowed the "gathering" of communities where not only do members not all know one another but in many cases none of them has ever been in the physical presence of another. Some have found this physical anonymity extremely liberating—"no one knows what I look like online." But I see in the Internet some dangerous tendencies toward dualism. Avoidance of some of the cultural baggage that our bodies elicit is one thing, but it is a short step to a complete severance of our bodily existence from our personal identities.

The Christian church, as much as it has been tempted toward dualism throughout its history, has also been provided with one of the most effective antidotes to this human tendency. Our insistence on the reality of the incarnation and the resurrection has been a powerful corrective to dualism. In the Gospel of John, the author confronts dualism almost immediately in the claim that "the Word became flesh and lived among us."[1] And at the end of the Gospel, we encounter the resurrected Christ inviting Thomas to touch his wounds and making breakfast for the disciples.[2] If we allow that Jesus is the "the first fruits of those who have died,"[3] then we find in Jesus' resurrection some interesting affirmations concerning our bodies. We know in particular that the individual context of our redeemed state will take place in a resurrected body.

There is much about this reality that is hidden from our view, but what little we do know has had a profound effect upon our behavior. The reality of the resurrection has prevented us from the twin temptations of dualism. On the one hand, we cannot indulge our bodies. We cannot let the passions of our bodies govern our every action and decision, but rather we must submit our bodies to the Lord. We are to avoid the fate of those whose "god is the belly."[4] On the other hand, we cannot deny our bodies through ascetic practices. Jesus was constantly correcting this false view of holiness in his life and was accused of moral laxity as a result.[5]

There are no simplistic answers to how we are to treat our bodies once we accept the implications of the resurrection, but the one thing we must not do is ignore our bodies. We have learned not to pit the "spiritual" against the "bodily" and focus our religious aspirations only toward the "spiritual." We have learned to counter this false spirituality with the biblical notion of submitting every aspect of ourselves (mind, body, emotions, etc.) to the lordship of Christ. As Christians we have had to learn to take our bodies seriously as part of our spiritual existence because our bodies most certainly are going to be part of our resurrected existence.

Now if we know that the individual context of our redeemed existence is going to be the resurrection body, what can we know of the communal context of our redeemed existence? For this, we look to the book of Revelation: "And I saw the holy city, the new Jerusalem, coming down out of heaven from God, prepared as a bride adorned for her husband."[6] Just as the resurrection body provides the individual context for our redeemed existence, so the resurrected city provides its communal context.

66

This renewed understanding of the resurrection city can, I believe, help us to counter some of the dualistic tendencies in our current society, just as the concept of the resurrection body helped the early church counter some of the dualistic tendencies of that time. On the one hand we cannot overstate the possibilities of our cities, as the public Christians tended to do during the last century. Creating the perfect, problem-free city will never redeem humanity. On the other hand, we cannot ignore our cities, as private Christians have done, by focusing our efforts as Christians solely on evangelism and stopgap acts of compassion while allowing our residential and commercial decisions to starve our cities of their life force.

Again, there are no simple solutions to how we are to live in and with our cities, but the one thing we must not do is ignore them. We must figure out how to work out our discipleship to Christ in the specific context of our cities. We must confront the problems of the city, such as overcrowding, addiction, and declining schools, and not run away from them to the sanitized world of the suburbs. And we also must enjoy our cities for the cultural performances, civic art, and opportunities for human interaction that they provide.

■ Receiving the City: The Stewardship of Culture and the "Built" Environmental Movement

The environmental movement in this country really came into its own following World War II and especially in the 1970s. While there was some concern for the environment earlier in the twentieth century—evidenced in the National Parks movement—a significant shift took place in the latter half of the century. We became aware as a culture of the fragility and interconnectedness of our natural environment. We realized that decisions that farmers were making about weed suppression could have a significant impact on songbirds in the wild, fish in the rivers, and even our children's milk. There emerged a new willingness to forgo efficiency and cost-effectiveness in production and consumption in order to protect and preserve our natural environment.

As our culture renewed its appreciation for the environment, the Christian church discovered that it had a unique voice to add to this movement. We learned that dominion had more to do with caretaking than with exploitation of the created order. We learned that the God whom we serve included animals in the Noahic covenant, restricted work for beasts in the Sabbath laws, and forbade the wasteful destruction of trees in the Deuteronomic laws.[7] And we learned that creation waited with us for the time when it would be freed from its bondage to decay.[8]

The shock wave of the environmental movement was felt in the Christian church most tangibly in a renewed appreciation for the idea of stewardship. We learned that stewardship has as much to do with our natural environment as it does with our personal finances. In particular we learned (or remembered):

1. that the created order reflects the glory of God and has inherent worth independent of our use for or appreciation of it;
2. that we did not create the natural world and we therefore must receive its benefits with humility and gratitude; and
3. that the created order is fragile and that we have a mandate to preserve it and care for it.

What if a similar revolution were to take place with respect to our built environment as has happened with our natural environment? Certainly our secular culture is moving in that direction. The preservationist movement is reminding us that our important buildings, despite being more fragile and perhaps not economically viable, provide vital links to our history and should be preserved. The New Urbanists are reminding us that human community requires a certain physical structure that has been provided in all times and all places of the world except in postwar America's sprawling suburbs. And now environmental and farm lobbies are discovering that urban sprawl is one of the greatest threats to our farms and wilderness.

There is a growing awareness that our downtowns, civic cores, and traditional neighborhoods are not only valuable to the overall health of our culture, but are also fragile and somewhat irreplaceable ecosystems. In some ways they can be compared to how we have come to understand rain forests in the last decade or so. We must preserve them now or realize too late the innumerable benefits we had been receiving from their existence.

But if our culture is going in this direction, is there a Christian voice to add to this conversation? Does being a covenant people of God give us a special mandate with respect to our built environment as it does with our natural environment? Is there a stewardship mandate for our cities? Certainly, as we have already noted, cities have had a mixed history in the history of salvation. Cities were initially a physical manifestation of our rebellion against God. But God took our rebellion and redeemed it for his purposes. In God's hands, the city became a place of redemption.

Now, there are some significant differences between the natural environment for which we have a clear stewardship mandate and the built environment of our cities. The natural environment was created more directly by God, while the built environment required more human participation. With the natural environment, it is easier to understand ourselves as receiving something that we did not create. However, because a living city cannot really be built by one community—in one generation—most of what we experience in and contribute to our cities is something that we did not create but have received. So just as our stewardship mandate for the natural environment begins with gratitude for what we have received directly from the Creator, so our stewardship mandate for the built environment of the city begins with gratitude for what we have received from our (divinely equipped) predecessors.

Another way that the cities in which we live are from God is that he has provided the vision and concrete hope for redemption in the city of New Jerusalem. As we witnessed throughout the biblical accounts, God continually led his people back to communion with himself within the context of a city. Had God not given John a particular vision of a city in his revelation, we may have been tempted to overlook the form of the city as the context for our redemption, and we may have missed something important in our cities. Because of this significant place in the history of our salvation, we cannot disregard the specific form of the city as a unique context with redemptive possibilities. John's vision gives us permission to examine our own cities for such redemptive possibilities, even if they exist only as a shadow form of what is to come.

Certainly, cities (in the historical sense of the word) are unique in many respects among the current options for human habitation. Cities tend to be relatively compact, allowing their residents to walk or take public transportation to get from place to place. Cities integrate residential and commercial use as well as types of residential living to provide lots of places to walk and a variety of types of people to see on the way. Cities can be places of great beauty, with their grand public spaces as well as sufficient patronage to support a variety of artistic endeavors. And cities can also be places of profound heartbreak, as gathering places for those who are not known or welcome in small towns and suburbs. Each of these unique features of cities provides particularly conducive settings for such Christian concerns as incarnational ministry, aesthetic appreciation, engagement in meaningful dialogue, and welcoming strangers.

But cities, as most of the world throughout most of history has known them, have been increasingly on the decline in this country since World War II. More and more we find ourselves spread out to the point that we spend far more time in our cars than interacting with our neighbors. Our residential life is highly segregated according to the slightest variations in income levels, and we have banished every commercial gathering space (such as coffee shops and restaurants) from our neighborhoods. We have constructed lavish private lives for ourselves and have abandoned even the most rudimentary forms of civic engagement.

The aggregate effect of each of these decisions has been the desertion of our urban cores and many of our traditional neighborhoods. I imagine that in time we will find these privatized worlds we have created for ourselves to be oppressively lonely and empty and will want to venture out for a walk around the block or a stroll downtown, only to find that there are no more blocks to walk around and that our downtowns have long ago been replaced with national-chain landscapes. If we wait that long, we may find that we have squandered away a treasured possession and that we will have a very difficult time bringing it back. But we're not there yet, and there is still time to reverse the trend. And to this end, perhaps we can extend our stewardship mandate to include our built as well as our natural environment.

■ Organic Cities: Living with Contingency as a Discipline of Spiritual Growth

If we as Christians want to take the physical structures of our cities seriously, at some point we must deal with the thorny issue of the future prospects of our cities. We need to acknowledge with the writer of Hebrews that "here we have no lasting city, but we are looking for the city that is to come."[9] And we have to take seriously the image in Revelation of the old heaven and earth passing away before the new heaven and earth are established.[10] The simple fact of the matter is that regardless of how engaged we are with our cities and no matter how our cities thrive, in the end they too will be destroyed and replaced with something better. So why should we put any effort into our cities if they are not going to last?

We are not the first ones to deal with this problem of sustainability with respect to the city. The exiles in Babylon faced a very similar dilemma. We are familiar with the admonition given to them by Jeremiah to "seek the welfare of the city where I have sent you into exile, and pray to the LORD on its behalf, for in its welfare you will find your welfare."[11] What may be less familiar to us is that the context of that command was a promise that the exile was to continue for seventy years. Seventy years is a long time, but it is not forever. And so the Israelites were commanded to work for the good of a city that was to be a significant part of their com-

70

munity life for the immediate future but not to be their permanent home. Whatever could God have had in mind with such a command?

Certainly turning Babylon into some kind of surrogate Jerusalem could not have been the purpose of Jeremiah's instruction. Perhaps what was being accomplished was the shaping of a people more than the shaping of a city—although the shaping of the city may have been an important means to that end. It is like when a mother and daughter decide to build a wooden boat together. What is really being built is a relationship more than a boat—although you couldn't just take the boat out of the equation and have the same effect. In the same way, God may have been building up his people in asking them to invest in and pray for the city of Babylon, but they could not ignore Babylon and expect to fulfill God's intention with them.

Rather than trying to determine what specific characteristics God was building into his people at that point in their history, let us move ahead into a New Testament context. In the New Testament we see the Holy Spirit as the primary agent involved in the formation of our character as God's people. And the fruit (or result) of the Spirit's work is: "love, joy, peace, patience, kindness, generosity, faithfulness, gentleness, and self-control."[12] In my experience, these characteristics are certainly not made manifest (and probably not formed) in the abstract, but rather come to light in specific situations that call for love, kindness, patience, and so forth.

Could there be a connection, then, between the eternal city as the form of our redeemed existence and the temporal city as the crucible in which character is formed for that eternal existence? Certainly, we see this negatively in people's decisions to reject the city. Cities force us to live, work, and play near people to whom we may need to show love, gentleness, and kindness. In the suburban ideal of a large home surrounded by a large lot, we don't ever have to see others, let alone interact with them. Cities are filled with physical, historical, and relational contingencies that require patience and self-control on our part. The suburban trend is to inflict standardized houses and standardized stores on an area, irrespective of regional history or local ethos, in order to maximize the efficiency of the builder and the spending power of the consumer.

Of course, cities do not guarantee the development of fruits of the spirit. In fact, the opposite is what we tend to expect. Cities stereotypically are known as impersonal, cold, and hostile environments. While some of these impressions are well deserved and accurate, many of them are false generalizations based on anecdotal evidence. After all, you are more likely to be greeted by name at the corner coffee shop on your block in New York City than you would be by the teenage employee at the Starbucks at the strip mall that is two miles from your housing subdivision.

71

Nevertheless, the point is that the conditions of city life create opportunities for the fruits of the spirit to grow if one is in fact being directed by the Holy Spirit.

Cities also require a certain kind of humility from those who decide to develop or live in them. Unlike the suburbs, where one solitary agent can design and build a large swath of land into a huge housing subdivision or megastore, cities grow organically as a result of the aggregate effect of thousands of agents throughout history on one particular area of land. Ironically, the organically grown city will in almost every case be more beautiful and interesting than the solitary work of subdivision or megamall, no matter how talented the architect or builder may be. It is an interesting and enduring testimony to how our communal life is so much richer than our individualized ideals.

It needs to be restated at this juncture that rural life is also a setting that requires a great deal of humility and communal values from those who live there. Certainly, the biblical witness and general observation would suggest just as much, if not more, potential for spiritual growth in a rural setting. As much as this is true, even this observation underscores the importance of our cities. For the past forty years Americans have been abandoning their cities, but they have not been fleeing to true rural settings. Rather, they are heading to the suburbs, where they push out the edges of the cities, thus destroying much of our farmland. The American Farmland Trust has estimated that we lose up to one million acres of farmland per year to sprawl.[13] It appears, therefore, that for direct as well as for indirect reasons, we have ample cause to invest in our cities, because we continue to find our welfare in their welfare.

So much of our Christian literature seems to be focused on the question of whether and how we can save our cities. It seems to me that we need to adjust this approach and begin to look for ways that our cities can save us. I mean *save* here not in the sense of salvation from sin—only Christ can do that—but rather save our souls from the damaging effects of uglification, standardization, privatization, and mass consumerism that have fueled this historically unprecedented appetite for sprawl in our country. But to receive the blessings that our cities (historic downtowns and traditional neighborhoods) can provide for us, we need to learn to see our cities once again.

We need to train our eyes to see the corner coffee shop and grocery in a neighborhood as the rare and beautiful species that they have become. We need to learn to stand back in awe at the broad, tree-lined avenue that has as a terminating vista a grand public building (a standard gesture of civic art in an earlier time but now deemed cost-ineffective). And we need to take advantage of the pedestrian-friendly setting of the grid-pattern layout with ample sidewalks by walking (alone or with our children), treating each corner as a fresh opportunity for exploration and adventure as we choose our route, instead of being directed from cul-de-sac to feeder road like some product on an assembly line. If we learn to see and even to love these urban features, we will begin to cheer when our cities and neighborhoods are preserved, and we will begin to weep when they are destroyed. We may even teach ourselves how to build and live in cities, as the rest of the world has been doing throughout history.

Part 2

Markers of the City

For he looked forward to the city that has foundations, whose architect and builder is God.

Hebrews 11:10

■ We've explored the history of thinking about cities in this country. We've examined what the Bible and theology suggest about cities. But we haven't yet defined what a city actually is. And it's not as easy as it first seems to come up with a good definition of a city.

What is needed is a definition that is general enough to include such diverse locations as Missoula, Seattle, and Mexico City, as well as Victorian London and ancient Jerusalem. But we also need a definition that is specific enough to distinguish between a city and a small town or a city and a suburb.

Raw population numbers do not provide an adequate criterion for determining city status. Federal Way is a municipality in the greater Seattle area with a population of over 83,000. But few of the residents of Federal Way consider themselves to be living in a distinct city. However, in Montana, where the state population is less than 1 million, a community of 50,000 residents can develop a strong sense of being an important city.

On the other hand, a checklist of specific physical attributes that we come to expect in a city seems to come up short as well. One might look for the presence of an airport, a professional sports stadium, a major department store, or some high-rise buildings to confer the status of a city upon a particular place. But many of the attributes that would be on our list today would be relevant only for this generation or in this country.

The most meaningful way that I have found to define a city is to say that you tend to know when you are in one. This sounds like a cop-out, but this is one area where I feel that our intuition might really be our most reliable guide. In the following section, we'll examine some of the general features that would indicate to the visitor that he or she is in a city. These features can be understood as six distinct markers of the city:

- public spaces
- mixed-use zoning
- local economy
- beauty and quality in the built environment
- critical mass
- presence of strangers

A city is a place that is characterized by these six markers. Not all cities are characterized by all of them. And there are some places that are not cities that may have some of these characteristics. A familiarity with these markers will give us handles upon which to hang our impressions of the communities in which we live, whether or not they qualify as cities. And they also will help focus and clarify our discussion about the merits of city life.

I've deliberately chosen to use the word *markers* rather than *principles* to describe these attributes. To call these attributes principles would imply that their purpose is to help in the creation of something that will be understood as a city. In fact, this is diametrically opposed to the purpose of compiling such a list. Almost every attempt to develop an ideal city from the ground up has been an absolute failure, whereas the greatest cities have grown up organically over centuries of human habitation. No one person (or community) can truly build a city in one generation. The best we can hope for is to understand what is good about the way cities do develop.

Understanding these markers may help us in our preservation efforts by bringing to light much that is good and valuable in our existing cities. These markers may help us repair damage that we have inflicted on our cities over the past half-century. And finally, we may find in these markers some wisdom that can be applied to suburban or even rural development.

Public Spaces and Incarnational Ministry

Wisdom cries out in the street; in the squares she raises her voice. At the busiest corner she cries out; at the entrance of the city gates she speaks.

Proverbs 1:20–21

In real life, only from the ordinary adults of the city sidewalks do children learn—if they learn it at all—the first fundamental of successful city life: People must take a modicum of public responsibility for each other even if they have no ties to each other.

Jane Jacobs, *The Death and Life of Great American Cities*

■ Public Spaces

There is a fifty-foot sidewalk in front of my house that runs perpendicular to my walkway. The sidewalk belongs to the city, but it is my responsibility to keep it clear of debris. If there has been any snow overnight, I am responsible for shoveling the sidewalk—by 9:00 A.M., according to the municipal code. I'm glad to do it, because this law makes sense to me. The sidewalk in front of my house is heavily traveled from about 8:00 A.M. to 5:30 P.M., mostly by university students. As I observe my "clients" on the sidewalk, I've noticed that most of them wear pretty sturdy hiking boots during the winter months, but some of them are in dress shoes, and others are on crutches or in wheelchairs. I think about all of these pedestrians and their needs as I shovel the loose snow and try to decide my strategy for dealing with the ice that has formed.

❧

In the afternoons when the weather is good, I like to take my daughter Kate to the park. It's about a three-block walk and provides a good chance for us to catch up on the events of the day. Kate's favorite activities at the park are the swings, the slide, and a climbing ladder that makes a 45° climb up to the play structure. There are six swings and two slides that Kate likes. Usually, Kate will be able to use either a swing or a slide when she wants to; however, every once in a while we have to wait our turn while another child enjoys it.

The climbing ladder is a little more complicated, because it is used pretty continually. There are the toddlers who slowly go up the ladder and sometimes go down. They have more enthusiasm than language skills or foresight and will start climbing without realizing that there is a child at the top starting to come down. And then there are the big kids who tear up and down the ladder in a game of tag. They usually have the sense to choose the side of the ladder that is not being used by another child as they flee their pursuer. And then there are the in-between-age kids, like Kate, who are trying to be fair and take turns but must make difficult judgment calls, depending on who else is on the ladder.

❧

On Saturday mornings in the summer, our family likes to go to the Farmers' Market downtown. We can catch the trolley about five blocks from our house and take it straight to the market. On the way there, we are an efficient little family unit—two adults, three kids, and a stroller. On the way back, however, we've got fresh produce in the stroller basket and bedding plants in the seat. One of us is juggling an infant, a diaper bag, and a sapling tree, and the other is tending to a couple of tired and hungry preschoolers. Invariably, as the driver holds the back door open for us, it is a community project getting us on and off the trolley. People are generally very nice about helping us out, and there are usually some very sympathetic parents riding with us.

❧

■ Loneliness in the Suburbs

These are three snapshots of my current life in Missoula. They are not very remarkable, except when I compare them to the month that I spent in the suburbs. The house that I was staying in was a beautiful house that sat on about five acres of land. In the morning, I would leave from the front door and get into my car—which was parked in the driveway. As I drove into town, I would adjust the immediate environment to my liking through the climate control and the tape deck of my car. I would park in the church lot and would go through the back door straight into my office. At the end of the day, I would drive back to the house and park in the driveway. After dinner I might read in the backyard or relax in the hammock. On my days off, I wanted to explore the area, but there was no place nearby where it was clear for the public to park, and every parcel of land seemed to belong to an individual. There was no town to visit, so I usually ended up at some restaurant or shopping center. My free evenings were usually spent watching a rented movie.

The main difference between the life that I lived then and the life that I now live is the presence or absence of public spaces. A public space can be defined as a domain that is not controlled by an individual or a corporation, but is open for everybody to use. Sidewalks are public spaces. Benches usually are public spaces, as are parks and plazas. Public transit is a kind of public space. Streets appear to be public spaces, but for the most part, we experience them from the private sphere of our cars, so they function as private spaces.

Public spaces provide the neutral territory that is necessary for the formation of informal relationships and for the building up of existing relationships. Without public spaces, it can be very difficult to develop new relationships or, in some cases, to encounter other people at all. I remember my stint in the suburbs as being a particularly lonely time of my life. I had recently graduated from college, and many of my friends had moved out of the area. I was working full-time for the first time in my life, and I didn't have lots of free time to meet my social needs. If I'd had a group of friends in the area, I could possibly have put together a rich and varied social life through the private spheres that each one of them would have occupied. But as it was, I was miserable—despite living in the nicest house I ever expect to live in—because of a lack of public space.

We seem to have forgotten the value of public space in this country. Until about fifty years ago, public space would have been the first priority in our building projects. The best spots in town would be reserved for plazas or parks adjacent to important, monumental buildings. And no self-respecting neighborhood would be without ample sidewalks. But

79

most of the postwar building efforts have shoved public spaces to the fringes, if they are included at all. Sometimes an out-of-the-way, odd-shaped parcel of land will be used for a park, and many streets in residential neighborhoods are built without sidewalks. We have trained ourselves to notice only the buildings in our communities—their size, number of rooms, and square footage. We no longer see the spaces between the buildings and their relationship to each other as of any importance.

This is the result, largely, of our love affair with the car. Our current building takes into account the needs of the car much more than it does the needs of the pedestrian. Where once there were front porches and inviting entryways, now there are two- and three-car garages that take up most of the frontage of our houses. At one time we built roads with sidewalks that were interesting and pleasant for the pedestrian; now we widen roads constantly, making it impractical and unsafe to even cross the street. Daniel Kemmis has observed that if the inhabitants of an alien spaceship were to view our cities from an aerial perspective, they would probably come to the conclusion that the sentient and relational beings in our culture are the cars, because everything is designed to facilitate the smooth operation of, and relationships between, our cars. Human beings, if noticed at all, would be thought of as the servants of these greater beings.[1]

We, as Americans, love our cars because the car represents much that is valuable to us as a culture. Our cars represent a high level of freedom and independence—we can go where we want when we want to in our cars. Our cars represent power—we are reminded of the triumph of technology over the limitations of nature when we turn the key in the ignition and hear the roar of the engine. And our cars provide a comfortable level of privacy—we don't have to talk to or be seen by anyone we don't want to as we fly by at sixty miles per hour.

As Christians, however, we need to acknowledge that none of these values—freedom, independence, power, or privacy—are held in very high regard in the Bible. Instead, the Bible encourages us to submit to one another in love, to serve one another in humility, and to value relationships—even with strangers—above all else. And in calling us to these values rather than to the values we have adopted as Americans in the twenty-first century, the Bible's writers really have our best interest in mind. Ultimately, independence, power, and privacy in their extreme forms lead us to a lonely and distorted version of human existence. It's time that we call into question the assumption that the needs of the automobile should be met above all else. We need to build cities and neighborhoods that allow us to get out of our cars and get to know one another by paying attention to the age-old conception of public space.

■ Sharing, Incarnational Ministry, and Discourse

As a social creature and as a citizen, I would care deeply about the creation and preservation of significant public spaces in our communities because of how they facilitate relationships among people. However, as a Christian, I find even more compelling reasons to be interested in the idea of public space. Public spaces require us to share with one another, they allow us to truly dwell among our neighbors, and they provide a context for a healthy exchange of ideas among a free citizenry.

Sharing

One essential quality of public spaces that is relevant to Christians is the necessity of sharing when we are in a public space. Public spaces force us to think about and interact with people we don't necessarily know. My life in Missoula is linked with college students, young children, and other families through the public spaces we share. Public spaces mitigate class differences—they are neither my turf nor your turf. And so they force us to relate to each other as equals.

The necessity of sharing creates the opportunity for learning about and practicing love. I don't always want to leave the warmth of my house to shovel the sidewalk for these students who walk by my house each day. On the other hand, there is nothing to prevent the fellow passengers on the trolley from scowling and rolling their eyes as our family struggles to get ourselves and all of our stuff through the door. As our children watch these interactions that I have with my community and practice their own interactions at the park, what they are learning, hopefully, is love. And as we talk about the love that God has for us and his desire that we love one another, these minor interactions provide the flesh-and-blood examples for our theoretical conversations.

Incarnation

Another potentially important quality of public spaces is how they provide a context for incarnational ministry. I sit on the local Young Life committee here in Missoula. Young Life is a para-church ministry that has revolutionized the way that the church looks at youth ministry. In particular, Young Life has developed and advocated what they call an incar-

81

national approach to youth ministry. By *incarnational ministry* they mean that we don't sit around the church and try to convince youth to come to us, but we go and "meet kids where they're at."

Young Life workers do a lot of "contact work," which means that they are at the high schools, at the sporting events, and at the malls, getting to know young people and building relationships with them. The Young Life leader then uses the relationship base that has been developed with a youth as a comfortable context to share Jesus Christ with that person. This incarnational approach to ministry has been a highly successful approach to youth ministry, and the church is slowly learning to emulate this model.

Incarnational ministry was not invented by Young Life. It is, in fact, the strategy that our Lord himself used with us. The Gospel of John tells us that the "Word became flesh and lived among us."[2] God was not content to remain far off and beckon us to come to him; he entered into our world and became one of us as a way to communicate his love. He not only came to us, but he dwelt among us. He lived his life in our midst and shared everyday activities with ordinary people.

The public spaces of first-century Palestine were an integral part of Jesus' ministry on earth and facilitated his incarnational approach with people. Certainly, Jesus spent time in the private spaces of other people's homes. He also ministered in the semiprivate realm of temple and synagogue. But by and large, most of his ministry took place in public spaces, where he risked relationship with people he didn't know and interacted with them on neutral territory.

One problem with taking on the suburban mentality as Christians today is that we can make it very difficult for ourselves to practice incarnational ministry. Can we really say that we are dwelling among even our neighbors when there is no sidewalk connecting our homes to each other and no park or plaza for us to bump into one another during our free time? If our normal, everyday activities rarely coax us out of our private spheres of home, garage, automobile, and office, how can we build relationships with those whom we don't already know?

Now, of course, if one is committed to an incarnational approach to ministry, one can practice it in any setting. Young Life thrives in many suburban locations. If a person is bold enough or committed enough, he or she will find a way onto the high school campus, the social circles of the shopping mall, or the parking lots of the minimarts to hang out with students. However, incarnational ministry is much more natural and comfortable in settings that have good public spaces.

Discourse

A final benefit of public space is how it can facilitate communal discourse. Perhaps we can approach this topic best by considering the issue of the mall. In many ways shopping malls have become the most enduring public space in American culture. And in many ways they function well as public spaces. They attract a variety of people of a variety of different ages, and they have sufficient common space for people to informally interact with one another. Malls can enrich community life by encouraging seniors to walk the mall before the stores open, by sponsoring rose shows and promotions for the local children's theater, and by providing a safe place for kids to trick-or-treat. But what malls cannot do is provide sufficient forum for the exercise of free speech and communal discourse.

As much as a mall functions as a public space, it is fundamentally a private commercial venture. Rose shows and school band concerts are one thing, but an antiwar folk singer or a group of antiabortion Christians is quite another.[3] Ultimately, if the use of the common area of the mall does not contribute toward the commercial goals of the management, it will not be allowed to persist. This is not to blame mall owners in the least. They are businesspeople who are accountable to a board of directors or stockholders and are given a particular mandate. However, it does provide a very good reason for us not to sit idly by while the mall becomes our only public space in this country.

As citizens of a democratic country, we ought to be very concerned that there is sufficient public space for expressions of free speech. I've seen Christians wearing gospel sandwich-boards at freeway off-ramps and at busy intersections because there is no other place to interact with the public at large. We must retain the right not only to speak our minds but also to have a viable audience. All members of a free society should desire this even if they might disagree with the point of view of whoever might want to express his or her views. And as Christians we especially ought to be concerned that there are adequate public spaces for us to be able to share the good news of the gospel openly as well as productively.

Already we show the effects of a deplorable lack of public space for these kinds of purposes. Since true public space for discourse has virtually dried up in the past fifty years, we have seen the emergence of some very poor substitutes. It appears as if public debate in this country goes on through the venue of bumper stickers, trash radio, and daytime talk shows. None of these venues provides real dialogue; rather, they reduce us all to very narrow and extreme camps on any given issue. They certainly don't convince anyone to think differently about anything, and they tend to bring out some of the worst examples of human interaction.

■ Praying for Sidewalks

It's not entirely true that we have forgotten about public space in this country. One does hear every now and again an impassioned plea for more parks for our children to play in. Or for more open space for recreation. But as Jane Jacobs reminded us forty years ago, parks are one of the most overrated types of public space and sidewalks are among the most underrated.[4] Some parks are used by people only four hours per day if they are used at all, and many parks (if they are underused) can be downright dangerous. But good sidewalks get almost continual use and can increase the safety of an area, provide a setting for informal contact, and assimilate children into the community's life. Before we conclude our discussion of public spaces, we will take one last look at the lowly sidewalk.

There is an Ace Hardware about a half a mile from my home. Typically, I find myself there a couple of times a week (or even a couple of times a day) depending on what kind of project I'm working on. I few years ago, I tried to walk to Ace with my daughter—who had just been born. She was fighting sleep, and the stroller always seemed to work when nothing else would. It was a beautiful day and I wanted to be out enjoying it and seeing people. On the first four blocks of sidewalk in my neighborhood, we had a lovely time. We saw people who had seen the "It's a Girl!" sign in our yard but hadn't yet seen Kate, and we talked to neighbor kids who were out enjoying the spring weather.

Once we crossed Higgins Avenue and got onto Brooks, however, everything changed. There would be a sidewalk for a block, and then it would end and we would have to traverse a parking lot. Then we would have to detour three blocks because there wasn't a sidewalk or parking lot—only landscaping that our stroller couldn't navigate. Not only did I become exhausted and frustrated, we didn't encounter a single person on the last seven blocks to Ace Hardware. No one had intended for someone to walk in this area. The sidewalks, where they existed, were just an afterthought by an individual business owner and did not create any sort of continuous walking path. I found myself at Ace, frustrated and tense, and decided from then on to take my car when I had to travel on Brooks.

Over the last few months, there have been construction crews going block by block and putting a continuous sidewalk on Brooks. I don't know whose idea this is or who's paying for it, but every time I see them link one more block to the next I give a silent cheer. I've even found myself praying for this project in my daily devotional. I don't know if I'm the only person in Missoula who is excited about this public works project—I'm pretty sure I'm the only one praying for it. However, as a Christian, I can't help but see how this small extension of our public space will not only improve our quality of life, but also allow us to have a greater impact in our community.

I feel blessed to be part of a community that seems to value its public spaces, not only by preserving them, but also by building new ones. I wonder about other communities that leave public spaces on the periphery of their municipal agendas, and other individuals who choose to live, work, and play in places devoid of public spaces. I know that in my life, even the most luxurious private sphere did not even begin to fill the void left by the absence of good public spaces that I now enjoy.

Certainly our lack of public space cannot be accounted for by a lack of resources. Many countries with significantly lower per capita income levels far surpass our achievements in terms of such spaces. Go anywhere else in the world and you are sure to see more beautiful and more accessible parks, plazas, and sidewalks. Is it that in this country we don't see the value of public spaces or that we lack the ability to create them anymore? Perhaps the necessity of communal consensus and individual compromise is beyond the scope of our current repository of civic energy. For our sake and for the sake of our children, I hope that it is not. Our lives will be poorer for having let this mainstay of human community pass us by in this country.

6

Mixed Use, Pedestrian Scale, and the Whole Person

Thus says the LORD of hosts: Old men and old women shall again sit in the streets of Jerusalem, each with staff in hand because of their great age. And the streets of the city shall be full of boys and girls playing in its streets.

Zechariah 8:4–5

The market experts . . . have been unrelentingly spreading the same message for over thirty years: build sprawl or lose your shirt. Specifically: do not mix uses; do not mix incomes; build walls and security gates; put the garages up front; and assume that nobody will walk.

Duany, Plater-Zyberk, and Speck, *Suburban Nation*

Freddy's Feed and Read

There used to be a book store/deli/coffee shop just two blocks from my front door, called Freddy's Feed and Read. It was the perfect place to enjoy a cup of coffee while basking in the morning sun or to pick up one or two ingredients for dinner on the way home from work. Because of its neighborhood location, you always saw someone you knew when you stopped by Freddy's. And there were always a few people gathered, having a conversation there. After the original owner of Freddy's died, some of the momentum for this neighborhood hub also died. Under new management, Freddy's wasn't able to turn a profit and eventually had to close its doors.

The owner of the building carefully selected a new tenant for the site. The main floor was going to be a family-run pizza place, and the top floor was going to be an annex for a well-established local coffee shop and bakery. To make this work, the owner had to apply for restaurant zoning to replace the deli/bookstore zoning. This change was challenged by the local homeowners association, because of concerns about increased traffic and noise levels, and eventually was brought before the city council.

Some other residents of the neighborhood put together a petition in support of this new venture, and I agreed to take the petition door to door on my street. Most of the neighbors on my street were willing to sign this petition, but a few politely declined. My neighbor across the street was one of the few who didn't want to sign the petition and, as we are on friendly terms, he felt that I deserved some explanation. "We just don't believe in mixing residential and commercial uses" is what he told me. From his perspective, then, not only was there a problem with this new venture, but even Freddy's had been a bad idea.

The prohibition against mixing residential and commercial uses in one particular area is a fairly entrenched practice within this country. It began innocently enough as an attempt to stabilize the real estate market. A potential homeowner didn't want to risk a purchase in a new area if there was a chance that in the future a pulp mill might be opening next door. Therefore, a tool known as zoning was developed to remedy this kind of a situation. Zoning involves specifying certain areas for certain kinds of uses. Originally, as we have noted, zoning was a reactive tool used to prevent specific situations of noncompatible uses in a particular area. Over time, however, zoning became a universal proactive planning mechanism used to separate every conceivable kind of use into a separate area.

This later stage of zoning laws is known as extreme separation (or single-use) zoning. Extreme separation zoning prohibits all commercial activity from residential areas. It separates single-family houses from multifamily buildings. It even separates large houses on two acres of land from slightly smaller houses on one acre of land. Over the years, extreme separation zoning has played a role (either intentional or unintentional) in both class separation and racial separation in this country.

And extreme separation zoning appears to have had an overall detrimental effect on our urban and neighborhood texture.

Whereas in the early stages zoning was a logical governmental response to citizen concern, in its current manifestation the connection to either logic or citizen concern is more tenuous. Certainly, zoning laws in existence in most cities today were not forged out of any kind of a public process, but were developed (or copied from a template) by engineers and city bureaucrats who care more about predictable patterns and neat categories than charm and neighborhood ethos. Regardless of how they came into existence, however, zoning laws should not be exempt from critical evaluation. It makes sense to have a law preventing a pulp mill or a slaughterhouse from moving into a residential neighborhood. But is it as clear that a coffee shop or a mom-and-pop grocery is detrimental to neighborhood life? Or is it obvious that apartments and single-family houses need to be far away from each other? Is it absolutely necessary that large houses be contained in exclusive neighborhoods? These are some of the concerns that will occupy the present chapter.

■ Mixed-Use Zoning vs. the Segregation of Use, People, and Time

The opposite of extreme separation zoning is known as mixed-use zoning. Mixed-use zoning allows a diversity of compatible uses to exist within a particular area. Residential situations that could be considered compatible for a mixed-use area would include large and small houses; apartment buildings and row houses; and apartments above stores and in outbuildings, as well as in small-scale public housing projects. Coffee shops, bars, grocery stores, gas stations, hair salons, banks, dry cleaners, and bakeries are just a few of the commercial ventures that could be included in a primarily residential area. For the most part, neighborhoods built before World War II allowed for mixed-use development, and neighborhoods built in the postwar era have tended to employ extreme separation zoning. In recent years, mixed-use zoning has been making a comeback in some newer developments.

To get a sense for how much use is mixed in your particular area, it is necessary to think in terms of a five-minute walk from the front door of your residence or your workplace. A five-minute walk is about a quarter of a mile, the distance that a typical person will choose to walk rather than take the car to get to his or her destination.[1] Within this five-minute walk, you can catalog the variety of residential and commercial buildings

88

in your neighborhood. A mixed-use neighborhood is one that has a great deal of variety within a five-minute walk, and an extreme separation sub-division will have virtually no variety.

An important feature of the mixed-use neighborhood is that it has a symbiotic relationship with public spaces. Mixed-use neighborhoods give people additional reasons to travel on or through public spaces by giving them interesting and useful destinations to which they can walk. A good network of sidewalks in a neighborhood is great, but without meaningful destinations, those sidewalks will be used mostly by early-morning or late-afternoon joggers or walkers. A charming park is a neighborhood asset for sure, but without commercial destinations nearby, it will be used mostly by parents with young children in the mid-morning or early after-noon. On the other hand, there might be a mix of uses between a strip mall and nearby condominiums, but without an adequate network of sidewalks, people will still take their car to get to the strip mall.

A neighborhood that has a mix of uses as well as a good network of public spaces provides for a richer experience of community than does one that is lacking in either or both. My neighborhood is somewhat mixed-use. I am fortunate enough to have a place called Grizzly Grocery five blocks from my house. In the morning, if we're out of milk, I often find myself making a quick walk to this store. On my way, I'm likely to see at least a few of my neighbors out beginning their day; I'll see the steady stream of college students running off to class; I'll pass the Christ the King Catholic Church and might say hi to Father Jim (one of my colleagues in campus ministry); I'll pass Great Harvest Bakery, where I'll wave to Diane (a member of the church who works there); and I'll note that the lights are off in Maarten and Lynn's storefront apartment and know that they've gotten an early start on the day.

That little trip to the store represents three ways that my life is enriched by living in a mixed-use neighborhood. I have the opportunity for incidental contact with my neighbors. I interact with people repre-senting a wide variety of ages and income groups. And I accomplish one of my tasks for the day without getting into a car. We will examine each of these advantages of mixed-use zoning in detail.

Incidental Contact

My wife and I have the distinct advantage of having both sets of par-ents living in the same city. As we began our married life in another city, we were committed to spending equal time and energy developing rela-tionships with both sides of the family. And we were grateful to avoid the problem that most of our married friends were having in trying to decide where to go for Thanksgiving or Christmas. We could always just plan a trip to Seattle and expect to spend time with my parents as well as hers. At first we thought that this arrangement meant that it didn't matter with whom we would stay when we were visiting, but we soon found out that it did.

No matter how many special dinners or walks or activities we planned with the other set of parents, we always felt that we grew closer in our relationship with the parents in whose home we were staying. A two-hour meal at a nice restaurant is memorable, but somehow the best conversations would take place late in the evening while getting a glass of water for bed, or in the middle of the afternoon while waiting for various family members to finish with their errands. What we discovered in the early years of our marriage is the unique value of incidental contact in building intimacy among people.

Deliberate contact with people is also extremely valuable. It is important to set apart special time and focus on developing particular relationships. But incidental contact builds relationships in an entirely different way. Incidental contact allows us to get to know people in their ordinariness and even in their pain. Jesus built much of his ministry around such incidental contact. Consider the story of the hemorrhaging woman:

> While he was saying these things to them, suddenly a leader of the synagogue came in and knelt before him, saying, "My daughter has just died; but come and lay your hand on her, and she will live." And Jesus got up and followed him, with his disciples. Then suddenly a woman who had been suffering from hemorrhages for twelve years came up behind him and touched the fringe of his cloak, for she said to herself, "If I only touch his cloak, I will be made well." Jesus turned, and seeing her he said, "Take heart, daughter; your faith has made you well." And instantly the woman was made well. When Jesus came to the leader's house and saw the flute players and the crowd making a commotion, he said, "Go away; for the girl is not dead but sleeping." And they laughed at him. But when the crowd had been put outside, he went in and took her by the hand, and the girl got up. And the report of this spread throughout that district.[2]

Jesus had not planned to meet this woman on this day. He had no deliberate strategy to begin a healing ministry for these kinds of disorders. And this woman was not likely to have felt confident enough to set up an appointment to meet with this famous healer. Nevertheless, because Jesus was on a public thoroughfare, he encountered this woman and she was forever changed.

Now, try to imagine this story in a contemporary setting. Jesus is in a private home in a subdivision, where he gets a call from an elder of the megachurch, twelve miles away, whose daughter is sick. He and his disciples hop into their Suburban and drive twenty miles across town to another subdivision and heal the elder's daughter. The other parts of town they encounter at forty MPH through shatterproof glass. The hemorrhaging woman is in one of these other parts of town, perhaps in a seedy motel, alone in her pain and convinced that she is not important enough for someone like Jesus.

Now, incidental contact does create occasions for this kind of dramatic encounter, but more often its significance is felt in more subtle ways. Incidental contact in its most basic form simply helps us to get to know our neighbors and build relationships with them. Of course, one can always invite one's neighbors over for a cup of coffee or even a meal, and many outgoing people do just that. However, for most people, inviting someone into one's home is a significant social risk and involves a lot of additional effort. Many Christians feel that they ought to invite their neighbors over but feel guilty about the fact that they haven't yet done so.

Ray Oldenburg acknowledges this kind of difficulty in his book *The Great Good Place*.[3] He claims that because it is such a social risk to invite a person into one's home (for both the host and the invitee), most people have some kind of screening mechanism that they will use before they attempt it. Usually, people have to know someone fairly well before they will invite them into their home. This restricts home invitations to work colleagues, people known through community associations, or perhaps next-door neighbors. Also, Oldenburg points out that most people's lives are busy with their work, their kids, or both. Inviting someone over involves coordinating schedules, cleaning the house, and preparing some kind of food. Because of these kinds of considerations, even highly motivated people have people over to their house only a few times per week at best.

In light of this limitation on our ability to get to know the people in our neighborhood, Oldenburg touts the value of the "third place." He claims that between the private worlds of work and home, we all need a third place to informally gather with our neighbors. This third place can be a coffee shop, a bar, a café, or even a barbershop. The important thing is that it is open to everyone, with no set times when one must go there or when one must leave. It is in this kind of setting, Oldenburg claims, that we can get to know our neighbors without the social risk of inviting them over. It's even possible, over time, to get to know the people in one's third place well enough to invite them over for coffee or a meal at one's house.

But even if contacts made in the third place do not lead to the intimacy of a shared meal at someone's home, the semi-intimate relationships that are formed in these settings have significant value for a neighborhood. Robert Putnam, in his book *Bowling Alone,* has described and evaluated this value under the rubric of social capital.[4] Social capital, Putnam explains, is the economic value of human relationships. It is comparable to physical capital (tools) and human capital (training). In places where social capital is high, for instance, crime is reduced, because people who know each other tend to look out for each other. Also, places with high social capital tend to be places where less money is spent on legal fees, because trust and communication take the place of contracts and litigation. And mixed-use neighborhoods, with an adequate third place nearby, tend to be places with high social capital.

Community

Another advantage of living in a mixed-use neighborhood is the wider experience of community that it provides. In the first place, it allows people from different income levels to live near each other and interact with each other. This is important, because in our contemporary society, people from different income brackets interact with each other only with some degree of paternalism on the one side and resentment on the other. In the best of circumstances, the rich interact with the poor only in the context of an activity that is meant to "help them" in some way. In most cases, those of widely different income brackets do not interact at all, and they see each other merely as categories and caricatures. In this light, there is immeasurable value in the simple conversation between a CEO and a janitor as they wait in line to buy the morning paper at the local grocery store.

This kind of contact not only widens the range of people with whom we interact, it also deepens the relationships that we have with individuals in our community. There once was a time when the school teachers, store clerks, and even the maids working in a particular community could also live in that community. So the person teaching your children at school would also be another adult role model that your children could see taking care of his or her yard or walking to church. Now entry-level teachers often have to find an apartment or starter home in a neighborhood far away from the one in which they teach. Extreme separation causes us to see people primarily as the function that they fulfill, rather than as whole people. And to see people solely within the framework of the function that they perform is to see them as much less than what God has created them to be.

This brings to light yet another advantage of living in a neighborhood that includes a good mix of residential types. The mixed-use neighborhood allows a person to go through a variety of life stages without moving to a different community each time. I was recently bringing communion to an elderly member of our church in her assisted-living apartment. As we were visiting, she pointed out the window to the house across the street. She explained to me that it was the house that she and her husband lived in for many years before he died and she moved to her current location. She also talked about the high school a couple of blocks away and how she attended that school many years ago.

In a mixed-use neighborhood, it is possible to get your first apartment, then move to your first home, perhaps move to a larger home as your family expands, and then finally move back to a smaller home or an apartment as the children grow up and move out. In most of the developments created after the Second World War, one would have to move to an entirely different part of town for each of those changes in life situations and would have to build an entirely new network of social contacts. As a result of these major transitions at each stage of life, the social connections that are developed in each area do not tend to run very deep.

One sees the effect of this even when it doesn't involve moving from one house to another. Many families choose to live in the suburban tract house development because it seems to be good place to raise kids. And it is, for a while. The single-use subdivision where each house is on a cul-de-sac provides a great environment for very young children. The cul-de-sac is a safe place to ride bikes, and the backyard is great for playing on the swing set or in the sandbox. But when the children get old enough to want to explore beyond their own homes and before they can drive, they often become restless in the single-use neighborhood. Whereas their mixed-use counterparts are being oriented to adult society by walking to the corner store to buy candy, stopping into the local barbershop to bring a message to Dad, or watching the mechanic fix cars, single-use-neighborhood kids are begging their parents to drive them to the mall.

Time and In-Between Time

Extreme separation zoning not only segregates types of buildings and people into different areas of the city, it also segregates the time in our day into unrelated bursts of activity punctuated by energy-draining car trips. Getting into the car and driving in the city or suburb is not considered to be an enjoyable experience for most people, and with young kids it can be quite an ordeal. Driving brings out the worst side of being human in us. Other drivers, instead of being neighbors whom we greet, are competitors with us for limited lane space and parking. Even people who wouldn't dream of saying an unkind word to another person's face will curse and even make rude gestures to other drivers when they are behind the wheel of their automobile.

It is no great surprise, then, that people want to spend as little time as possible driving their cars. The way that we have generally sought to achieve this goal has been to try make our car trips faster by widening or adding traffic lanes, timing traffic lights, and streamlining roadways. But rarely do we consider the possibility of helping people to spend less time driving by eliminating the number of car trips that they need to make in their day. In fact, many of the solutions that focus on helping us to drive faster or more efficiently actually make it harder to choose to walk to a destination.

The result of the auto-oriented culture that we have built for ourselves is that our days feel fragmented into disjointed elements, and we are forced into the role of harried tour directors who must create complicated itineraries for ourselves and our families. The pieces of the day with which we have to work consist of time at home, where we often feel as if we are missing out on the action, time shopping or running other errands, social time where we see other people, and personal improvement time, where we exercise or take in some kind of culture. Each of these nodes of activity is split up by in-between time in which we sit and drive our automobiles. When every element of our being human and functioning in a human environment requires a separate trip in the car, it is no wonder that even the most laid-back personalities complain of life's frantic pace.

On the other hand, in the mixed-use neighborhood a simple trip walking to the store can meet multiple goals. It is primarily an errand to purchase food for the family. But it is also exercise and an opportunity to get some fresh air, while being reminded of the time of day and the season of the year. It can be a social occasion if you happen to meet a neighbor on your way to the store. And it can even be a culturally enriching experience if your neighborhood includes beautiful public buildings, public art, or street performances.

This kind of qualitative difference between mixed- and single-use areas can be seen in our places of work as well as in our places of residence. My church is just across the river from our downtown hub. If I need to run an errand or buy lunch, I will often choose to walk downtown instead of jumping into my car. I have found almost without fail that two things happen when I make this choice. The first is that I always seem to run into at least one or two persons who were on my list of people to call for that day—making the rest of my day that much less busy. The other is that I seem to run into someone who was not on my to-do list that week, yet nevertheless was someone whom I needed to see as a pastor. Either they had stopped coming to church and I hadn't noticed or they had some kind of news to share that I would otherwise have missed.

Also, when I walk downtown I notice the weather and the status of the river more than I would in my office or from my car. I see church members who work downtown and wave to them through the window and am thus reminded of the worlds these people inhabit outside of the church. In short, my working day always seems more enjoyable and more integrated when I make a trip downtown. Compare this to many contemporary office parks in the middle of nowhere. Employees in these settings can choose between eating in the cafeteria or racing in their cars to find some fast-food place miles away.

The mixed-use neighborhood or commercial area gets us to use our sidewalks by giving us meaningful destinations. It provides us the opportunity to interact with a broader range of people than we would normally throughout our day. It allows us to experience people not only in their professions, but also as neighbors and fellow citizens. And it allows us to have more integrated and fulfilling days—both for us and for our children. Having seen all these advantages of the mixed-use neighborhood, why are they illegal in most zoning codes? Of course, even with such advantages some people will prefer the single-use neighborhood. But does it make sense to make the single-use neighborhood the standard pattern of every new development? It seems time to reevaluate this practice and consider a return to the kinds of mixed-use neighborhoods that had been such a vital part of city life for generations that preceded ours.

■ "Walking by Faith" and Pedestrian Scale

Having the option of walking to our daily destinations not only improves the quality of our lives and deepens our experience of community, it also connects us to the biblical setting where walking was a part of life. Not only did biblical role models like Moses and Elijah or Jesus and Paul do a lot of walking as they lived their day-to-day life, but much of the language they used implied a life of walking:

Happy are those who do not follow the advice of the wicked, or take the path that sinners *tread,* or sit in the seat of scoffers.[5]

Those who *walk* blamelessly, and do what is right, and speak the truth from their heart . . .[6]

He has told you, O mortal, what is good; and what does the LORD require of you but to do justice, and to love kindness, and to *walk* humbly with your God?[7]

If we say that we have fellowship with him while we are *walking* in darkness, we lie and do not do what is true; but if we *walk* in the light as he him-

95

self is in the light, we have fellowship with one another, and the blood of Jesus his Son cleanses us from all sin.[8]

They said to each other, "Were not our hearts burning within us while he was talking to us *on the road,* while he was opening the scriptures to us?"[9]

. . . for we *walk* by faith, not by sight.[10]

In fact, many of the literal walking references are taken out of our translations, because walking as a mode of transportation has so diminished in our culture:

In view of the richness of the language, it is a pity that most modern translations of the Bible replace the image of walking with more prosaic descriptions such as "live," "behave," or "conduct yourselves." While not inaccurate, these translations cut off any imaginative associations that references to walking conjure up. As a result, the already weakened possibility of everyday activities becoming windows to divine realities is diminished even further.[11]

Besides the advantages of the mixed-use versus the single-use neighborhood, there are many other features of our cities and neighborhoods that can encourage the practice of walking. These features are usually included under the general heading of what is known as pedestrian scale. There is actually quite a bit known about what makes for a comfortable and interesting walking environment. It is just that for the most part, we as a culture have not valued the practice of walking enough to pay much attention to these things.

We will examine just a few basic features of pedestrian scale here. One aspect of pedestrian scale is known as *enclosure.* Enclosure explains why one can walk for blocks down a tree-lined street or a typical main street pleasantly, while covering the same distance navigating the parking lots of the huge, boxy, chain retail stores is exhausting. One generally likes to walk where the environment feels like an outdoor room or a hallway, where the space is defined by walls.

This effect is achieved by having the right ratio of building height to street width. Experts in pedestrian scale estimate this ratio to be about 6:1. The distance from storefront to storefront cannot be more than six times the height of the buildings without losing that sense of enclosure.[12] Most zoning codes require a certain setback for newer buildings (to allow for parking) and make this kind of enclosure impossible to achieve. In residential areas where the buildings cannot gracefully sustain the 6:1 ratio, a uniform line of trees can create a similar effect and make for a pleasant walking experience.

Another feature of pedestrian scale is *visual interest.* A person has to have something interesting to look at—to engage in as a human being—in order to enjoy the experience of walking. The unbroken horizontal plane and huge signs of the "box" retail stores are built to be seen from great distances by people driving cars and offer nothing of interest to the pedestrian. Huge skyscrapers are designed to impress passing motorists or to look good on a postcard but do nothing for the lowly pedestrian unless the first floor is designated for retail space. To get a sense of this, note the difference walking in the financial district of a large city versus the retail area. Or consider the endless sea of garage doors in most modern subdivisions, which give no evidence of human habitation to the passing pedestrian. Conversely, in older neighborhoods, people walking can peek over low fences to see interesting front yards, welcoming front entrances to homes, and picture windows giving evidence of life being lived within. And in downtown areas where storefronts go right to the sidewalk, people tend to enjoy going for a stroll.

Lastly, a person needs to feel *safe and protected* when walking. Streets where parallel parking is allowed provide a comfortable barrier of parked cars to protect the pedestrian from the rush of traffic on the street. Streets that are twenty-five feet wide (as opposed to forty feet) give the pedestrian a much more comfortable experience of crossing the street. The system of cul-de-sacs leading to curved feeder roads encourages cars to travel at speeds that are unsafe for pedestrians, while the grid pattern of traditional neighborhoods causes automobile traffic to move more slowly and gives pedestrians a fighting chance.

Pedestrian scale can be a precise science for those involved in planning and building. But it doesn't have to be. Almost anyone can easily tell the difference between a place where they enjoy the experience of walking and a place where they simply choose to take their car to cover the same distance. The value that we, as a culture, place upon walking bears a complementary relationship to the pedestrian scale of the places that we inhabit. The more we value the practice of walking, the more we will demand pedestrian scale in our built environment. And the more areas we build with a sense of pedestrian scale, the more we will find people choosing to walk to their destinations.

■ Seeing Negative Space

Because of my interest in the city and its physical features, people often ask me what I think of a new building going up in our city. And I usually find that I cannot answer the question very well. I may have some kind of an opinion about the style or quality of the building, but what I really feel about its contribution to our civic life has as much to do with the spaces between the new building and the surrounding environment. The fact that it is set back one hundred feet on its lot to allow for parking in front does not escape my notice. Nor can I ignore the fact that there is no convenient way to walk from this building to the building next door. I also consider whether there is a good mix of other kinds of businesses within the immediate vicinity, so that someone could use the services housed within this building without adding one more car trip to his or her day. Because I am aware of the value of mixed use and pedestrian scale, sometimes it seems as if I see everything *but* the building in evaluating whether I like a particular building.

In the book *Drawing on the Right Side of the Brain,* the author encourages the reader in a similar kind of exercise.[13] She calls it drawing negative space. For example, instead of drawing an object, like a birdcage, by reproducing its shape and the detail of the metal bars and perch, the author advocates drawing the spaces between the metal bars and the space around and outside of the birdcage. This practice teaches our eyes to see everyday objects in an entirely different light and opens up our creativity.

I propose that we could all benefit from learning to see the negative space within our cities and neighborhoods. Generally, when we evaluate a building we see square footage, room layout, and parking. Sometimes we might see aesthetic value or visual interest. What I am suggesting is that we need to train ourselves to look at how a building sits on its lot and how it relates to adjacent buildings and the area as a whole. If we can learn to see buildings this way, we will value places that encourage the kind of community we want to experience. And we might even recover the lost art of building places that sustain a more satisfying human environment.

7

Beauty, Quality, and Other "Nonessentials"

Finally, beloved, whatever is true, whatever is honorable, whatever is just, whatever is pure, whatever is pleasing, whatever is commendable, if there is any excellence and if there is anything worthy of praise, think about these things.

Philippians 4:8

It will no longer do to say that virtue is too complex to be understood—and that, therefore, we prefer no definition of virtue to a possibly imperfect one. In restoring these notions of value to respectability, we may even resurrect the fundamental source of beauty in our world, which is the shame, the original sin of our innate human imperfection.

James Howard Kunstler, *Home from Nowhere*

■ Buildings That Matter (and Buildings That Don't)

The Missoula Children's Theatre (MCT) is the largest children's theater in the country. Every year they bring twenty different full-scale children's musical productions to about six hundred locations throughout the world. In addition to this ambitious traveling schedule, they put on six adult and three children's shows for the local community at a quality level far beyond what is typical for a community of this size. MCT is housed in the Central School building, which is a beautiful old brick structure in the heart of our downtown. About three years ago, they completed a $4 million expansion to the building, which established a permanent stage for MCT shows, while at the same time creating a new Center for the Performing Arts. This addition of new performance and rehearsal space has been a jewel in the heart of our community, providing a high-quality venue for drama, dance, music, and visual arts.

At the opening gala for the new theatre and center, I spoke with George Lambros, who owns the real estate firm that played a key role in the preservation of this important building. He recounted a scene that took place eight years ago. The school district had closed Central School and had sold the building to the Missoula Redevelopment Agency until a permanent buyer could be found. It had been on the market for some time without any solid offers, and so George and an invester began making plans to raze the building and put in an automobile servicing mall based on a very lucrative model that they had seen in another city.

It was at this time that Jim Caron, the executive director for MCT, approached George about using the building for his children's theater. Realizing that this building was a community building and that MCT was a valuable part of this community, George tabled the plans for the auto mall, which freed up the building to be sold to MCT. It meant passing up a good business opportunity, but he understood the concept of a building that belongs to the community. George had previously been involved in a similar project, which helped to turn the old Carnegie Library Building into the Art Museum of Missoula. He also had a personal stake in the Central School building, having attended school there as a child. And on the night of the opening he was one of the thousands in the community who were glad for his wisdom and community spirit. Not only did a permanent home allow MCT to grow and thrive over the years, but also a building of beauty and quality had been preserved in our community. Furthermore, the community had access to this building both as artists and as patrons of the arts.

A few years prior to these auspicious events, another building's fate was being decided. In a different part of town, on Brooks Street, the building that for twenty years had been the home of the retail chain Best was being demolished to make way for a new Safeway. The old building was a simple and cheap brown box that was put up in the early 1980s. People in the community noted this development only because it meant that they could get 70 percent off at Best before the building was destroyed, but I never heard one word of remorse over the demolition of the building. In fact, when I went to City Hall to determine the exact date of its demolition, I could find no record of when it was built or who built it and no one in the office who could remember much about the building.

In any given community, people seem to know which buildings matter and which buildings don't. Buildings with some history to them matter to people in the community. Beautiful buildings designed by a local architect for a local context are valued much more highly than the standardized structures that are dropped onto the community from the central office of a national chain. And buildings that are built with pride and a certain level of quality evoke a feeling of pride and ownership within the local populace. Communities are not always able to preserve these buildings that matter, but they value them nonetheless. And it is in cities that so often these buildings that matter are to be found.

The third marker of the city, then, is the beauty and quality of the built environment that can be found there. This can include buildings built by private companies that become important landmarks for a city, such as the Chrysler Building in New York City. It can also include grand public buildings like city hall, the post office, or the county courthouse. Even public projects like rose gardens or monuments become part of the local beauty. Nonprofit organizations like churches, universities, and theater companies contribute to the beauty of a built environment as well. And homes, ranging from the grandiose to the quaint, especially in older neighborhoods and in the downtown core, are often a source of community pride. Finally, the very act of planning the layout of the city itself—known as civic art—provides a source of beauty that can sometimes go undetected because it is so indirect.

To be sure, cities are inconsistent when it comes to these features of beauty and quality in the built environment. And cities are not the only places where beauty is to be found. Some cities are filled with beautiful structures, and some cities seem to have sprung up without giving aesthetics a second thought. Beauty and quality in the built environment are not exclusive features of the city—there are beautiful churches, county courthouses, and homes in rural settings as well. But in general, it is the older historic cities in this country that have the relatively high concentration of beautiful buildings, other structures, and layout. And it is also true that many of our newer cities and subdivisions are conspicuously lacking in such examples of beauty. Civic beauty is concentrated in our older cities because they were built in a time when beauty and quality were more highly valued by the public, labor and material costs were cheaper, and there was sufficient concentration of population to support and enjoy such ventures.

■ Beauty, Quality, and God?

One question that we must consider, in this context, is whether God cares about such things. Does God care about beauty and quality on this earth and in our cities?

This question is too general for our purposes. There is ample evidence of God's valuing of beauty in the creation itself: "The heavens are telling the glory of God; and the firmament proclaims his handiwork."[1] The question is not whether God cares about beauty, but rather, does he care whether the things we create are beautiful? Subsumed under this general question are two other questions. The first has to do with whether we even can create anything beautiful. How can beings who are sinful and imperfect hope to approximate anything even remotely related to that which God creates? The second question has to do whether we should spend our time trying to create beauty. Why would God want us to be distracted with a temporal thing like beauty when we have such a clear and urgent mandate for evangelism? It seems more logical that God would have us simply be grateful for the salvation of our souls and leave the creation of beauty to himself.

It would seem logical, if this were so, but this perspective on beauty is not characteristic of the God we meet in the Bible. I discovered this quite unexpectedly when I was beginning my work on the city and at the same time was reading my way through the Old Testament. I had just gotten past the familiar territory of Genesis and the first half of Exodus. I was preparing myself for a long stretch of obscure detail throughout the remainder of Exodus and into Leviticus. But this time, I was struck precisely by the detail of this section, which I had previously overlooked:

> You shall make a curtain of blue, purple, and crimson yarns, and of fine twisted linen; it shall be made with cherubim skillfully worked into it. You shall hang it on four pillars of acacia overlaid with gold, which have hooks of gold and rest on four bases of silver.[2]

Since I keep my Bible on an end table that also contains many of our magazines, I had to do a double take to make sure I hadn't picked up *Martha Stewart Living* by mistake. No, this was, in fact, God's word. I was reading from Exodus the account of God's instructions to Moses concerning the construction of the tabernacle. Mind you, this isn't even the temple yet—this is the temporary tabernacle, which would be carried through the wilderness for forty years. Later, God would provide even more extensive instructions for the creation of the permanent temple.

From this passage, God clearly cares about how things look—not only things that he makes, but things that we make also.

If God cares what things look like, then God can be honored by the work of a skilled craftsman. Later, this point is confirmed as God begins to describe the vestments for the priests:

> Bezalel and Oholiab and every skillful one to whom the LORD has given skill and understanding to know how to do any work in the construction of the sanctuary shall work in accordance with all that the LORD has commanded.[3]

God made a special point to give these two artisans the ability to create things of beauty. It shouldn't surprise us that God provides what is necessary for the creation of beauty that is pleasing to him. God not only appreciates that we can create something of quality that is beautiful, he specifically equips certain persons with the skill and understanding to create such things.

Now clearly, this example of God's instructions for the tabernacle is historically unique and cannot be applied indiscriminately to our entire built environment. In the first place, this tabernacle is the locus of communion with God for God's chosen people and not easily comparable to the Chrysler Building. Second, this tabernacle is the prototype for what is to become the temple in Jerusalem, which later becomes obsolete at the moment of Christ's crucifixion.[4] We will have to return to the issue of the general nature of our civic buildings and the wisdom of putting effort into things that are temporal. But for now, let us proceed with the understanding that God can be honored in the beauty of things that we make with our hands and that, furthermore, God has gifted people with the specific ability to make things beautiful with their hands.

■ Clouding Our Vision

When we ask a broad question such as that of the value of beauty, we're sure to come across the problem of the subjective nature of beauty. What is beautiful to me may not be beautiful to you. So what is the relative value of a neo-Gothic building versus one that is built in the Arts and Crafts style? These are important issues and have been the subject of long-standing debates among people who care about the beauty of our built environment.

For now, we will leave the constructive question of what form beauty shall take in our cities to the experts, and will instead focus on two movements in this country that have had a particularly destructive influence on the beauty within our built environment. The first, modernist architecture, has been a deliberate design movement that has tried to change the shape and look of our built environment. And the other, bottom-line economics, has been a general tendency to build without much concern for design. Interestingly enough, these two movements, which on the surface look to be very different, have had a very similar effect in eliminating beauty from our cities and neighborhoods.

Modernist Hubris

The term *modernist architecture* can have a variety of meanings in a variety of contexts. When we use this term, we are not intending to include all contemporary design styles that have emerged since the twentieth century. Nor do we even mean to include all design styles (spanning roughly from the 1920s through the 1980s) that could be considered to be part of the modernist movement. For our purposes, we will be using the term *modernist architecture* to refer to the later and more severe examples of the larger modernist movement. This kind of modernist architecture is known by names such as Bauhaus, brutalism, and International Style. What these forms of modernist architecture seem to have in common is

- a disregard for historical reference,
- a lack of ornamentation, and
- a lack of concern for legibility.[5]

Modernist architecture was born out of a *disregard for history*. The early part of the twentieth century was a time of great optimism and hope based upon technological advancement and a blind trust in progress. Old things were thought to be flawed, obsolete, and decrepit, whereas anything new was assumed to be superior to the old. And so the old was simply ignored. This was seen in buildings as much as anywhere. With modernist architecture, much of the organic vernacular that had been developing over centuries of building practices was cut off. A structure built under these principles ceased to be a collective expression of the patterns of human habitation that had developed over the years in that particular place, but rather became an attempt by an individual to make a supremely original statement.

This antihistorical trend in architecture tended to encourage and even reward pride and arrogance in the architect. And it also made for some uniquely oppressive environments for both living and working, because it ignored both the past (which had been preserved in traditions) and the present (which was expressed in the collective wisdom of the community). The biblical witness stands in clear opposition to both of these trends. Not only does God oppose the proud,[6] but it is also clear that pride brings contention and strife.[7] It requires humility and patience to study the context (historical, architectural, and geographical) and to design a building that fits into that context while making a positive contribution to it.

With regard to the basic value of history, God's people were rarely chastised for not being progressive enough but were condemned because they failed to remember. The Israelites were commanded to place twelve stones at the border of the Promised Land to remind them that it was God who faithfully led them there and not their own effort.[8] Remembering is a component of almost every aspect of our relationship with God. God's people were told to "remember this day" at the exodus and were instructed to "do this in remembrance of me" at the Last Supper.[9]

Now admittedly, the stakes are significantly lower when we ignore the history of architecture in our building practices than they are when we forget the history of our salvation and our covenant life. However, it's not too difficult to find within the wisdom literature some concern for honoring our history in a general sense: "Hear, my child, your father's instruction, and do not reject your mother's teaching; for they are a fair garland for your head, and pendants for your neck."[10] It is for this lack of basic wisdom that the modernist movement in architecture is gaining subsequent generations' concensus that it was a complete failure.

The second feature that characterizes modernist architecture is its *lack of ornamentation.* Buildings constructed in a modernist style lack graceful arches, ornate windows, and stately columns. Such buildings tend to have large flat walls, plain windows, and simple corners—not for the sake of simple elegance, but almost deliberately to be oppressive to the eye. This plain style in modernist architecture comes from two sources. The first is an attempt at solidarity with the factory life of the working class. There is strong socialist influence in modernist architecture, which creates an uneasy feeling about designing different kinds of buildings for different classes of people. And so rather than making factories more beautiful, the modernists designed upper-income homes and office towers that were as ugly as any tire factory.

The second influence on this plain style of building was a desire to be more honest. Most elements of ornamentation on traditional buildings (arches, columns, and vaults) were born out of necessity. Each of these devices were feats of engineering that allowed buildings to stand taller and contain more open space. But with the invention of modern building materials such as reinforced concrete, these techniques were no longer necessary. It was thought by the modernists that an arch was dishonest if it wasn't really holding up the roof. And so they loved to show the concrete blocks and steel girders in all of their brutal reality, as a way of being honest.

With regard to the egalitarian motivation for creating ugly buildings, Jesus rejects such abstract notions of social engineering on behalf of the poor. When a woman came to Jesus and poured expensive perfume on his head and feet, it was Judas who declared that such extravagant expressions of devotion were a crime against the poor.[11] It is not that the poor do not matter and so we should just indulge ourselves in whatever way that we please. Rather, the issue is that we do not take seriously human beings who happen to be poor when we reduce them to machines needing only food and water. People of all classes need beauty and dignity in their daily lives. My father-in-law was a pastor in the Philippines for a number of years. He recalls that it was the foreigners who used to complain about the beautiful cathedrals that were such a "waste of resources" among people of such abject poverty. But when you talked to the Filipinos, it was these very cathedrals that gave dignity and joy to their lives.

As far as honesty goes, the fact of the matter is that human beings like to look at arches, columns, and vaults. Human beings find unbroken vertical and horizontal planes oppressive to the eye, and windows without visual interest tiresome. The fact that honesty is an issue at all attests to the fact that the architect can see the building only as some kind of personal artistic expression rather than as something that belongs to the community that uses it.[12] Creating unsatisfying human environments for the sake of honesty is nothing more than putting a righteous spin on a basically self-indulgent practice. Architecture is "the profession of designing buildings and other *habitable* environments."[13] To ignore those very features that make our buildings habitable for the sake of some abstract ideal is in some sense a betrayal of the vocation.

Lastly, we consider the issue of *legibility.* Buildings not only protect us from weather, but also communicate with us. There is a kind of language in architecture that we are usually able to read. Architectural language can tell us about a building's use. In traditional architecture, a barn, a gas station, a warehouse, and a church all have a distinct form that tells us about their use. Architectural language can tell us something about the importance of the functions that go on within the building. A cathedral or a county courthouse will typically be more grand than will an auto repair shop, a private home, or a retail store. Architectural language can communicate a particular mood within a building. A particular building can be whimsical, grave, or reverent, depending on its use. Finally, legibility can tell us about the various features of a building. There is architectural language that can indicate to us where to find the front of the building or the main entrance, and how to navigate the inside of the building.

Buildings designed in a modernist style often disregard such conventions of legibility. Modernist architecture delights in jumbling forms of buildings with their uses. There are all kinds of examples of important civic buildings that look like warehouses and places of worship that look like office buildings. It is very difficult to determine anything about the relative importance of a modernist building on the basis of its architectural language. And a modernist building can be very difficult to access and navigate. The design of such a building seems to revel in hiding the front of the building, the door, or the stairway from the uninitiated.

I'm not exactly sure what the philosophical reasons are for avoiding such gestures of legibility in modernist architecture. Perhaps it's just one more way to thumb one's nose at history and convention. In any case, the effect on someone trying to use or access the building is one of inhospitality, distance, and sheer mockery. For a people with a mandate of hospitality, intimacy, and kindness, it is hard to see much that is redeemable in these kinds of modernist buildings. So it is as a Christian that I find these tendencies of modernist architecture extremely problematic.

In one sense, modernist architecture is simply one more style that has emerged within architecture over a long history in the development of that discipline. And we can be glad that as a particular style it seems to be on the decline. However, this design style seems also to have been a symptom of a deeper problem within the architectural community. The style seems to have been especially potent for expressions of a kind of hubris among those who subscribed to its tenets. Modernist architecture did not mark the beginning of hubris in the architectural profession, but it created a wedge that seemed to divide the architectural community into two different approaches to their craft.

On the one hand, there were architects who saw their primary role as that of visionaries and artists whose job it was to move humanity in new and unprecedented directions through their radical designs. On the other hand, there were the architects who understood their role to be that of public servants whose job it was to interpret the memory and the hope of a particular people into a coherent physical form that fit in with the rest of the cultural context. Modernist architecture as a design style seemed to introduce a moral distinction between those who practiced their craft from a position of pride and those who did so with humility.

If pride entered the scene in the guise of modernist architecture, it was greed that, ironically, produced very similar results through the influence of bottom-line economics. It is to this story that we turn next.

Capitalist Reductionism

Right in the heart of downtown Missoula is a beautiful old brick building that currently is the home of the Bon Marche department store. It was built between 1882 and 1891 as the home of the Missoula Mercantile, which was largest retail enterprise from Salt Lake to Seattle.[14] It is not an architecturally significant building, but its elaborate ornamentation is visually pleasing, and the quality of its masonry construction and its cast-iron storefront give it a sense of dignity and permanence. It is an important anchor for our downtown and always seems to make it onto the itinerary for our out-of-town guests.

In 1994, on the fringe of town, another building was constructed. This building was to house the Costco retail chain. Like the Mercantile, Costco was meant to be a retail hub for the region. This building has no pretensions to grandeur or permanence. It is a fifty-thousand-square-foot box that was constructed in a few weeks. Its heating system was flown in by helicopter, and its design is virtually indistinguishable from any Costco anywhere in the world. The only stylistic features of this building are the two familiar paint colors and the Costco logo, which can be seen clearly from the freeway. It fits James Howard Kunstler's assessment of most shopping centers today:

> Shopping centers hardly qualified as buildings in the historic sense of the word. Rather they were merchandise distribution machines that came in boxes that resembled buildings.[15]

I don't think that there is anyone in Missoula who would call the Costo building beautiful, and it does not contribute in a meaningful way to our built environment.

Suffice it to say that Costo does not make it into many tours of Missoula. I was lamenting this fact in a class and someone responded that in each generation only a few of the best buildings survive. According to this theory, every generation produces many ordinary buildings and a few grand ones. It looks as if old buildings are of a higher quality only because they were the exceptional ones that survived. It's an interesting theory, but I don't think that it would hold up to scrutiny. If Missoula can be seen as a typical city, it certainly disproves this theory. I don't think any of the buildings built within the past fifty years in Missoula would be worth touring now or fifty years from now.

Whenever this stark contrast in the quality of buildings built today versus those that were built a century ago is mentioned, someone is sure to bring up the point that no one could afford to build such quality buildings today. But is that strictly true? Sure, labor costs are a lot higher today than they were a century ago. But we are far wealthier, in terms of real dollars, than we were in the 1880s. At some level, the explanation for this difference must have something to do with the fact that corporations are less motivated to build beautiful, quality buildings than they were in an earlier era. What accounts for this radical shift in corporate priorities over the last century? At least three changes can be discerned.

In the first place, more and more corporations are *publicly owned* than they were a century ago.[16] A privately owned business can afford to care about such "peripheral" issues as dignity and integrity. A publicly traded corporation is ultimately accountable to its stockholders, who, in general, care only about the bottom line.

This bottom-line perspective explains perfectly why the Costco building looks the way it does. This building provides maximum square footage at minimal cost, and its design serves the simple purpose of easy identification for the consumer. The aggregate stockholders do not particularly care if this particular Costco continues to exist in Missoula in five years. If it doesn't prove profitable within a short period of time, a helicopter will come and take the heating system away—just as it brought it in—and the building will be scrapped.

The second change that has occurred is that *consumer values* have shifted over the past century. In a culture dominated by the corporation, we have assimilated the language and values of corporations into our individual and family lives. We have learned to be "efficient" above all else in our use of time. And we have learned to make financial decisions for our personal and familial lives according to a rigorous cost-benefit analysis. We have learned to expect the best value for our dollar and to ignore such issues as dignity and integrity.

Somehow in this process we seem to have lost our appreciation or concern for quality and beauty in the buildings that we encounter in our daily lives. It can be difficult to determine which is the cause and which is the effect in this situation. Either we have been so focused on getting value for our dollar that we haven't noticed or cared that the buildings being built today are consistently uninspiring, or we have raised two generations of Americans on such ugly standardized buildings that we have ceased to notice or care what our buildings look like.

The last factor that may account for a change in our building practices is the *change in venue for advertisement* over the last century. In the 1880s a corporation's building was an important means of establishing the strength of its product. The style of a building could show its occupant to be modern, traditional, or stylish. A permanent and quality structure could show that the corporation that built it was planning to stick around and back up its product. Today, corporations depend more on mass media advertising to achieve such goals.

This brings us close to an explanation of why we think that we can't afford to build buildings like they used to. The short answer is that we *can* build such buildings. It is just not cost-effective to do so for a public that has largely ceased to care about beauty, quality, or permanence. Corporations *will* spend one million dollars on a thirty-second advertisement during the Super Bowl. Corporations will gladly pay millions upon millions to have their products worn by superstars or to have them "placed" in a major motion picture. And Costco will spend money enough to build several beautiful buildings on mass distribution of junk mail.

Thus, it is a tradeoff more than a question of what we can or cannot afford. As consumers, we used to get beautiful, interesting, and inspiring buildings like the Chrysler Building in New York City. Now we get interesting, effective, and funny advertisements during the Super Bowl. The question is whether we are happy with the trade. What are the implications of slowly losing buildings of any worth in our contemporary culture?

■ Civic Art: The Communal Function of Aesthetics

The question of what we've gained and what we've lost with our diminished interest in aesthetic value is one that applies not only to our commercial buildings but also to our public buildings. A public that has learned to get the most value for its discretionary income will demand the most value for its tax dollars as well. And so we will explore this question further, through the lens of a public building.

Jury Duty

Last spring I was called up for jury duty. Early on a Wednesday morning, I had to make my way downtown to the Justice Court to fulfill my civic duty. The Justice Court is located in the Missoula County Courthouse. This building, which was built in 1910, is on the National Register of Historic Buildings and is considered to be the crowning achievement of the prominent Missoula architect A. J. Gibson. It is a beautiful neoclassical building that has "terra cotta walls on 3-foot-thick granite bases and an Italianate tower with an interior 2-ton bell on top of a large centered dome."[17]

It was inconvenient to serve on jury duty that day. I had a lot of work that I was supposed to accomplish that morning, and because I was going to watch the kids for the afternoon, we had to scramble to find child care.

The clerk at the Justice Court explained that I would be reimbursed twenty-five dollars for my service, which would hardly cover the cost of the child care. But I knew that the strength of our democratic system is the trust that it places in ordinary citizens like myself. It is a privilege to govern ourselves through exercising our right to vote and to maintain justice by serving jury duty. I knew that the collective goal of democracy was far more important than my personal vocation and our child care costs on that day, and I was glad to play my part.

I believe that this notion of the priority of the collective good over my personal desires was strengthened by the extravagant grandeur of that public building in which I was to serve my jury duty. I couldn't quite put my finger on it that day, but I believe that I was impressed by the notion that if the public good is important enough for three-foot-thick granite walls, then it is important enough for me to put aside my personal agenda on that day. Certainly there are others who don't share these sentiments. Juror #15 never showed up and never bothered to call in. And if anecdotal evidence counts for anything, I'm sure that there were many people called for jury duty who were able to make up acceptable excuses.

I have not charted the trends, but I wouldn't be surprised if there are more and more people finding reasons to avoid jury duty today than there were in earlier generations. It certainly seems that way. For people so accustomed to basing all of their personal and familial decisions on a strict cost-benefit analysis, it must be harder and harder to justify spending an entire day deciding the fate of a complete stranger.

If our participation in jury duty is hard to track, a trend that is easy to observe is that our public buildings have suffered terribly under the tyranny of reductionist economics. One would be hard-pressed to find a county courthouse or any public building built since about the 1950s that has any enduring value. In Missoula, our new sheriff's office and IRS building are built with the same care and quality of any boxy chain retail store.

I fear the subtle impact our recent building practices might have on future citizens of this country. I cannot help but make a connection between our awful civic buildings and our shameful record of civic participation, evidenced in our record of both voting and serving jury duty. Buildings reflect the values of a community, and they also influence them. Winston Churchill once said that "we shape our buildings and then our buildings shape us."[18] We tend to think of this notion in connection with grand and beautiful buildings like the English House of Commons. But what kind of imprint is being left on our character as we continue to build and patronize buildings such as Costco? It is to this question that we turn next.

Aesthetic Values

Having now looked at some of the factors that have led to an increase in the number of ugly buildings in our culture, let us explore some of the values that are reflected and shaped by the particular form of ugliness with which we are confronted each day.

One aspect of many of our modernist and cost-effective buildings is that they lack *human scale*. Human scale has to do with the elements that make a building or place relate to human size. The elements (doors, windows, ceiling height) are sizes that can be easily comprehended by the eye and seem accessible for human operation. Human scale does not feel too big or too small to an individual person.[19] Modernist architecture, with its massive planes of unbroken space, provides no detail for the eye to grasp a sense of space and proportion. And cheap, boxy, chain retail stores, with their oversized garish signs, are designed to be seen from an automobile at a speed of sixty miles per hour rather than by the lowly pedestrian. Once inside either of these types of structures, the individual human feels small and insignificant next to the massive heating ducts and steel beams. One doesn't feel like a human being capable of great achievements or tragic failures, but rather like one dispensable piece of a larger machine.

What is at stake with regard to human scale is nothing less than the doctrine of humanity. In the biblical witness, human beings are the crowning work of God's creation.[20] Of course, we are not perfect, and we are capable of acts of evil far beyond the rest of the animal kingdom. But we are anything but insignificant. Despite what these buildings make us feel, we are more significant than our cars. And we are more valuable than our buying power. Sometimes we need to be dwarfed by grand buildings that remind us of the priority of the collective good over the individual. But even in that situation it is our rampant individualism that is being tempered, while our basic humanity continues to be honored.

A second, related feature that most of our postwar buildings lack is *human imprint*. Human imprint has to do with the evidence in a building that a particular human being left his or her mark on a structure. This could be the influence of an architect who individually designed a particular building. It could be reflected in the brickwork of a particularly gifted mason. And it could even be discerned in the use of a particular type of stone that can be quarried only locally. Human imprint was deliberately avoided in most of the buildings that were designed in the International Style in the heyday of the modernist movement. And human imprint is almost never seen in the buildings erected by chain retail stores.

These buildings are designed at a national office and are constructed according to a standard template in all regions.

What is at stake with regard to human imprint is the doctrine of vocation. We know that whatever we are called to do, we are to "render service with enthusiasm, as to the Lord and not to men and women."[21] The kinds of working situations that are created out of standardized plans and uniform construction limit the potential for true enthusiasm in our work. We place a very limited value on craftsmanship in our culture, and we are losing people who can practice such crafts. We know that we are to think about "whatever is true, whatever is honorable, whatever is just, whatever is pure, whatever is pleasing, whatever is commendable" and anything that has "excellence" or is "worthy of praise,"[22] but we are finding ourselves increasingly stuck with buildings that are hardly worthy of such contemplation.

Civic Art

It is not just the individual buildings that have become standardized and ugly; the very layout of our cities has become less beautiful in the last half of the twentieth century. A dreary practice that is now the exclusive domain of engineers and traffic experts used to be a noble and beautiful tradition of civic art. Civic art has to do with trying to express a community's values and way of life through the layout of the city. Parks and squares would be placed in prominent spots to allow people to congregate and enjoy they beauty of their city. Boulevards would be beautifully landscaped, and major streets would terminate at the most important public buildings to accentuate their role in the community. The heights of buildings would be deliberately regulated to provide a proportional and harmonious skyline.

In our current situation, as long as traffic flows smoothly, no one seems to care about the visual or communal impact of our cities. And in some ways this loss of civic art is more detrimental to the quality of our public life than is the ugliness of the individual buildings. The haphazard and incoherent layout of our cities not only makes them uninspiring to look at, but also limits the ways that we can access our cities. And it limits the ways that we can interact with one another. This situation is most unfortunate because we know how to do it better. Civic art as a human discipline had been developing for thousands of years, and it is only in the twentieth century that we completely dropped it as a practice. Fortunately, if we ever renew our interest in this art form, we will have a rich repository of knowledge from which to draw. But the question remains as to whether we will ever renew such an interest.

■ Smokestacks in the Church

From a Christian perspective, then, perhaps there is particular value in beautifully designed and quality-built structures set within a coherent and eloquent city plan. Such civic treasures bring pleasure and delight to our daily lives, and they nurture in us communal and civic values. Cities that respect human scale honor the dignity of our humanity, and cities in which human imprint can be found honor the dignity of our vocations. Where inspired civic art has provided definition to the divergent elements of a city, a venue is provided for us as individual Christians or as communities to express our values and beliefs to our neighbors.

However much we might agree that civic beauty is important, such thoughts often come across as so much wishful thinking. Whenever I try to make a case for beauty and quality in our built environment, I encounter nods of approval but also a sense of resignation. "It would be nice, wouldn't it, if we could do things like they used to if only we could afford to" is the kind of statement that I've come to expect. I've tried to explain how in real dollars we are actually far wealthier today than when most of our beautiful public buildings were built. But somehow this line of reasoning seems too abstract to make any difference, especially when it comes to a discussion of spending any extra money to make our church buildings beautiful and quality additions to our cities.

My latest strategy has been to show a picture of an old factory with five smokestacks belching out black smoke. I then ask my audience to imagine a situation in which there exists some legal loophole that allows us to heat and power our church facility by employing the device shown in this picture. This setup would save us thousands of dollars in heating and power bills every year. Do you think that we as a congregation would go for it? I ask them. And they invariably agree that we would never do this—even if we were permitted to—because of the pollution, the ugliness, and the smell. We wouldn't want this kind of environment for ourselves, and we wouldn't want to inflict it upon our neighbors.

I believe that most congregations would answer in a similar manner. Certainly, people have lived with and near factories for years. It is not absolutely necessary to avoid this kind of a setup for us to function as a congregation in a neighborhood. It is just that we have broad consensus that this is not the kind of community life that we want for ourselves or that we want to communicate to our neighbors. And we are willing to incur higher costs in order to avoid this kind of setting. Why, then, is it so often considered extraneous to hire a competent architect or to use quality materials for the purpose of making our church buildings beautiful and elegant? Perhaps the degrading effect of smoke in the air is imme-diately apparent, whereas the impact of ugliness and the loss of human scale and human imprint are more subtle. Wherever our culture is on these issues, we need to think seriously about the values and truths that are conveyed by our church buildings and make sure that they are bib-lically and not just culturally informed.

8

Local Economy and the Permanence of Place

For where your treasure is, there your heart will be also.

Matthew 6:21

A community is not something you have, like a pizza. Nor is it something you can buy, as visitors to Disneyland and Williamsburg discover. It is a living organism based on a web of interdependencies—which is to say, a local economy.

James Howard Kunstler, *The Geography of Nowhere*

■ Economics, Ministry, and Continuity

About six years ago, we started a new campus ministry at the church. Among the initial group who became part of that ministry were a dozen college seniors who were regulars at our midweek worship service and provided a strong leadership base for the ministry. In May, when these seniors graduated, all twelve of them moved to Seattle to find work. Not one of them stayed on in Missoula, because there were no jobs. It is typical in campus ministry to use the recent graduates as leaders and mentors for the program, but we've never had a graduate stick around long enough to experience this.

✎

In my first six years in ministry, I probably have officiated two dozen weddings. Of all of the couples that I have married, however, not one of them is still around and involved in our community. Every couple eventually had to go out of town to find work. As a church community, we've never had the opportunity of walking alongside a couple during the crucial first years of marriage.

✎

I meet lots of people who don't mind being mobile and who expect to move around a lot as they become established in their careers. However, more and more, I am finding young people who want to live close to their parents as they begin to establish their own families. And I meet parents who want more than anything to live close to their adult children in order to offer support and encouragement as they raise their own children. Again, most young people in Missoula do not have the option of staying in Missoula and raising their families. There are not enough entry-level jobs here. There are some jobs in Missoula, but young people who want to return here must go somewhere else to get established in a field, and then, later, they can take a major pay cut and make a lateral move to Missoula. There are many families that have made that choice over the years, but it is less than ideal.

✎

The proverbial small town is supposed to be a good place to raise kids and to be a family. The irony is that most small towns do not have an adequate job base to provide opportunities for a family to stay for more than one generation. The reality of the small town, then, is that when the kids grow up they have to move somewhere else to raise their own families. A small town therefore often fails to meet the intergenerational requirements of true community.

Ironically, it is in the larger cities that things can be quite different. Currently, my three siblings live in the Seattle area—very close to where we grew up. My two brothers live in the same neighborhood in which we were raised. Their kids are going to the same schools we went to, and during the summer, they swim at the same beach we used to. They live four and five blocks from our parents, respectively, and are involved at the same church. My siblings have stayed in Seattle because they want

117

to be close to family and because there have been job opportunities that have made it possible to do so.

A third marker of the city, then, is a local economy. A local economy is one that is healthy enough and diverse enough to offer employment opportunities for a wide range of people in a variety of life stages. Small rural towns and resort areas (even when they are doing well economically) rarely provide enough jobs to support a multigenerational population.

A local economy is one marker of the city that Missoula doesn't fully exhibit. We do have a fairly healthy economy, with a major university, the U.S. Forest Service, and the health-care industry providing an adequate job base. What we don't have is a diverse economy. We lack sufficient entry-level jobs for our college graduates. We have lots of minimum-wage jobs—which offer little opportunity for advancement. And we have a small number of career jobs for those established in their fields.

A year ago, I had one student who really wanted to try to make it work. He had recently graduated from the university with a moderate level of debt. He liked the church community and the area, and so he decided to look for work. After an arduous search, he found an office job and felt lucky to have beat out some others for the position. He soon discovered that the salary of $14,000 per year was not going to allow him to meet even basic living expenses and to pay off his loans. After talking to some others who have been with the company for eight years and were not making much more, he decided to move to Portland to find work.

This weakness in our job market in Missoula is not only hard for the individuals who have to leave town to find work, but is also hard on those of us who stay. One of the things that I love about my position is the breadth of my responsibilities. I can be involved in a young person's life from seventh grade through twelfth, and I can be involved in the lives of their parents and grandparents through other areas of my ministry. However, to lose people in their twenties because of the economy is a constant source of frustration for me as well as for the church as a whole.

This lack of continuity is more that just sad for those who have invested in relationships with young people; it also presents a significant barrier to effective ministry. Just at the time when young people could really benefit from pastoral advice and mentoring from the older members of the congregation, we have to ship them out of town so they can find work. Paul advised Timothy to continue with those from whom he learned the faith:

> But as for you, continue in what you have learned and firmly believed, knowing from whom you learned it, and how from childhood you have known the sacred writings that are able to instruct you for salvation through faith in Christ Jesus.[1]

In Missoula, because of our economy, it is all but impossible for young people to continue in what they have learned in the context of an active relationship with the person from whom they learned the faith. The presence of a strong local economy would greatly improve this situation.

■ Local Culture

Every city has a personality—an identity—and a local economy can play a key role in enhancing or destroying that identity. If a local economy is stagnant or nonexistent, the identity of a city can become atrophied. On the other hand, if the profit motive alone provides the raison d'être for the local economy, the identity of a city can become standardized and sterile. The ideal situation for forming and maintaining a city's identity is one where there is broad communal involvement on the part of the citizens, clear vision on the part of the leaders, and a local economy made up of business owners who are invested not only in making money but in participating in the community.

The identity of a city can form and deepen the identity of its inhabitants. It can provide roots that remain with a person even when they no longer reside within the city of their origin. This idea is assumed in the biblical narrative with its descriptions of Jesus of Nazareth and Paul of Tarsus. Certainly, such local identification did not explain everything about an individual and often needed to be challenged. Nathaniel, after all, had to learn that some good could come out of Nazareth. Nevertheless, the place in which a person's identity was formed was assumed to have an enduring imprint on his or her personality.

In our current culture, this connection between identity and place is being lost because we no longer seem to understand the importance of place. With the onslaught of chain retail stores and large-scale standardized housing developments, it can be hard to discern any distinguishing characteristics of a particular city. A person could be placed in any number of housing developments or commercial districts throughout the country and have no idea whether he or she was in Houston, Tacoma, or Baltimore.

Our cities are losing their identity because the new structures that we build lack character or human imprint. And every time we lose one of our older buildings, our communal identity is impoverished. The husband-and-wife team of Lennard and Lennard, from the International Making Cities Livable Council, observes the inherent danger of this phenomenon:

The architecture of the city embodies the city's memory. When a building is destroyed then the memories that each individual had in connection with that building can no longer be passed on to others. And when too much of the original texture of the city is replaced by inappropriate structures our own memories fade. . . . If too much of the architectural heritage is destroyed, the city's communal memory of its unique identity is violated, making it susceptible to social problems.[2]

It's important to note that we are not talking here exclusively about the public buildings of a city—which are supposed to shape and reflect the collective values of a community.3 In the vast majority of cases, it is the private commercial buildings that become important to the identity of a city.

I experienced this first-hand when I was serving as a hospital chaplain one summer in Seattle. I had tried to prepare myself for the kinds of pastoral issues that I might encounter going from room to room in a large hospital in a cosmopolitan setting. I expected to encounter a challenging range of medical, cultural, and religious issues that would push me to the limits of my experience and knowledge. What I wasn't prepared for was the pastoral significance of the fact that the Frederick & Nelson department store in downtown Seattle was closing its doors that summer. I heard countless stories from patients who had bought their wedding dresses at Frederick's or had always gone there with their mothers to buy back-to-school outfits. The community was grieving the loss of a communal memory that was associated with that beautiful building.

Fortunately, although the Frederick's department store was going out of business, the building was not scrapped. It was bought by Nordstrom Inc. to be their flagship store in Seattle. Now, of course, Nordstrom is a chain retail store that has done its share of standardized building throughout the country. But the Nordstrom family is from Seattle and probably grew up with a love for the Frederick's building. They didn't keep up every one of the traditions that had been associated with Frederick's, but they did save the building and retained an important part of our communal memory.

This raises an interesting issue. Do locally owned and operated businesses invest more in the local culture than do businesses that are part of a national chain and managed from a remote location? Insofar as buildings make up the local culture, it would seem that this is so. In Missoula, most of the interesting buildings with personality are occupied by locally owned businesses, while almost every chain store is built according to a standardized plan and contributes nothing to the local culture or identity of Missoula. And it is the locally owned businesses that give Missoula its particular charm.

But what about the other aspects of the local culture? Do locally owned businesses contribute more than chain stores do? Certainly, chain stores have learned the value of investing in the local community for good public relations. One chain store has contributed computers to the local school district. Another chain sets apart a place where class supply lists are posted for the various elementary schools. And one chain welcomes preschoolers for field trips. The chains tend to focus their community participation on the schools because it's clearly a good cause and because it develops a relationship with a potentially very lucrative customer base. I'm not criticizing these stores for their desire to foster good public relations partially from a profit motive. Rather, I want to highlight how a locally managed business can do a better job supporting the local culture regardless of the profit motive.

It is hard to overstate the pride and ownership that the Missoula community has for the Missoula Children's Theatre. When MCT is getting ready to open a new show, there will be a publicity poster in almost every storefront window and tickets will sell out early. Often MCT staff will go to the community to borrow the props needed for their current offering, and they usually have no problem securing whatever they need. In fact, there are a number of local businesses with whom they have reached a standard agreement on this practice.

There was one show a few years back for which MCT needed a few items that the local import market didn't stock. One of the employees then decided to try the national chain import market in town. The manager of the chain store was cordial but taken aback by the request. He explained that the inventory is carefully monitored by the national office and that all charitable contributions had to be cleared by a separate department at the national level. Eventually, after several trips, the store did allow MCT to borrow one or two items for that particular show. But because it was so inconvenient, they have not done so since.

The issue here is not about being cautious with one's inventory or about wanting to be proactive with community contributions. What this account demonstrates, rather, is that local culture consists of the various elements that are particular to a specific locale. And it is the very specific and particular nature of these kinds of community assets that makes it very difficult for nationally owned and operated chain stores to help support them. The national chain stores have to pick causes to support that are general enough to work within any and every community in which they have a store.

This evidence for this pattern is anecdotal, and there are probably many exceptions that could be cited. But if one begins to look for examples, it is interesting how many can be found. I've taken to reading the advertisements in the playbill for MCT shows and have noticed that almost never will a national chain be listed as one of the sponsors of a particular show. It's not that the managers of local stores are more generous than those of the national stores, but rather that they know that there are certain causes and institutions that have specially captured the hearts of the local people, and that is where they want to invest.

■ Exchanging Commodities, Exchanging Relationships

Last Christmas my wife bought me a new sport coat. Rather than go to some megastore, she decided to go downtown to Desmond's—a locally owned men's clothing store. After Christmas, I was in the store getting the coat altered and was talking to Bill—the owner of the store. He was telling me how he had just bought snow tires for his daughter's car because she had to drive back to her university after the break. I was looking for snow tires also, so I asked him where he goes, and he told me that he always goes to Roemer's, just down the street.

Later that day, I went to Roemer's to see about snow tires and saw about five or six employees there, most of whom looked to be married and settled in Missoula. So I could construct a fairly realistic picture of where dollars went when Liz bought me a sport coat. Part of the markup went to Desmond's operations budget, and part went to Bill's paycheck. Of the part that went to operations, some went for rent and maintenance in a beautiful old downtown building, and some went to MCT to pay for an advertisement in the next show's playbill. Of the part that went to Bill's salary, some of it was used to buy new tires at Roemer's. The markup and service charge for the tires went to the employees at Roemer's, who probably bought lunch downtown or got braces for one of their kids at a local dentist. You can see how a dollar from our family, spent locally, circulates throughout the community, supporting the local culture and helping maintain one more opportunity for a person to stay connected in Missoula rather than move on.

Compare this scenario to one in which we buy a sport coat at Wal-Mart. At Wal-Mart a tiny fraction of our dollar goes to the paychecks of the salesclerk and cashier—who are probably students making minimum wage. Some of our dollar is going to a manager, who may have been hired locally but is more likely to have been transferred from another store in the region. If the latter, that manager may spend his or her money locally but represents the transitory, not the permanent, segment of our community. And most of our dollar will go to the corporate office and to the stockholders who are scattered throughout the nation and the world.

Don't get me wrong; I am not trying to be provincial. I am not suggesting that people who live in Missoula deserve jobs and paychecks more than do people who live elsewhere. Nor do I think that large corporations are necessarily evil. I'm sure there are many fine and outstanding people who are stockholders in Wal-Mart and count on revenue from their portfolios to meet their daily needs.

All that I am suggesting is that we might want to see our personal economic decisions as tools that we can use to impact our communities in positive ways. Just as we vote for a superintendent of public schools who we feel will help give our kids the best education possible, so we might want to buy our Christmas presents in a way that will give our kids opportunities for jobs in town after graduation or that will make our city a more interesting and enriching place in which to live. To do this, we simply need to widen our perspective on economic decisions.

Our tendency is to think very narrowly in our economic decisions. We compare prices, and if we can get the same product for even a slightly lower price, we will do so. What we need to learn to do is to take one more step and say "What else is being impacted by the purchase of this product?" The Christian community has demonstrated the power of this kind of thinking on other issues. There have been numerous campaigns to get certain convenience stores to stop selling pornography. Christians have been successful in getting stores to pull certain magazines off their shelves by threatening to not shop at their stores. What I'm talking about is less confrontational—I'm not suggesting we picket Wal-Mart. But we need to recognize the power of our economic decisions.

It is not the case that we always need to make an economic sacrifice by paying more for a service or a product in order to support some abstract communal goal. Often, when we learn to shop with communal concerns in mind, the benefits we receive are immediate. This is because so much more is going on when we purchase a product or a service than an exchange of money for merchandise. There can be a deeply relational aspect to our economic activity that can greatly enrich our commercial transactions.

Daniel Kemmis recalls an experience of shopping at the Farmers' Market in which he discovered this reality. He recounts the story of Lucy, whom he had known as a graduate student in Missoula. He remembers her graduation, where she announced that she wanted to start an organic farm, and how impractical it seemed to him at the time. And then, twenty years later, as he buys broccoli from Lucy (who is now running a very successful organic farm), he realizes that "as Steve weighs my broccoli and Lucy counts my change, the whole history of their farm and of our friendship is part and parcel of what we exchange."[4] Not only does he remember his role in the beginning of her farm, he recalls that she was one of the first to encourage him to run for mayor. Now, Kemmis could have gotten broccoli at Safeway for a few cents cheaper, but I'm almost certain that his exchange with the cashier and courtesy clerk would have been somewhat less profound.

As Christians, we can assess our economic decisions not only for the jobs and local culture that they support, but also for the relationships that they build. Stores and enterprises that are locally owned and operated are a deep part of the identity of those who are involved with them. As we shop at local stores, we come to know the owners and their stories, and they come to know us and our stories as well. This creates greater opportunities for us to impact our communities as Christians, and it is a much more enjoyable way to complete our daily tasks.

Just a few weeks ago, one of our church members went to buy me a new outfit as part of Pastor Appreciation Month at our church. She happened to go to Desmond's to pick it out. Somewhere in the process of trying to select a size, she mentioned whom the gift was for. Because I had shopped at Desmond's a few times before, Bill knew who I was and also happened to have my measurements on file. This created an opportunity for this church member to talk about her relationship with God and with the church, as she gave an account of what would motivate her to buy such a gift. Who knows what kind of impact this transaction may ultimately have, but I do know that our family's economic decisions as well as this church member's have allowed us as Christians to build some relationships outside of our church community where they didn't exist before.

It can be difficult to make a case for a local economy when the general trend seems to be moving toward a global economy. It is easy to be dismissed as being quaint—and totally unrealistic—when suggesting that we buy our broccoli at the Farmers' Market and clothes at the downtown men's store. It's hard to envision this ideal on a macro level without succumbing to cartoonish images of the medieval town and feudalism as the only political and economic models that would allow such a vision. It is, however, possible to develop this idea in a rational and realistic manner if we consider the model of a two-sector economy.[5]

In a two-sector economy, we divide our economic decisions into those where we want to encourage a local economy and those where we want to encourage a global economy. In areas where the potential for craftsmanship, personable service, and community investment is high, we might choose to pay a bit more for a locally made or distributed product. This might apply to a decision about food, furniture, clothing, health care, education, or instruction in music, the arts, or sports.[6] In areas where we want the most advanced technology and impeccable safeguards, we would favor companies that produce on a global scale.

Albert Borgmann provides three tasks that are best left to the global economy. The first is the maintenance and improvement of the infrastructure of transportation, utilities, and communication. The second is the production of certain goods and services, such as machine tools, cars, appliances, raw materials, insurance, and finance. The third is research and development.[7]

Of course, there are many more details to be worked out, but the two-sector economy provides a useful framework for restoring dignity and meaning to many of our commercial transactions.

■ Prospects and Limits of Capitalism

In this chapter, we have explored ways that local businesses play a key role in the development and maintenance of local culture. Local businesses provide jobs that allow people to remain in a particular place for generations. They tend to build the buildings that matter in a particular community, or they occupy and maintain those buildings through their rent. They can support local culture by donating products or purchasing advertisements. And they often provide a deeper relational component to many of our daily tasks.

There is another, more general way that local businesses support local culture. They provide the tax revenue and capital that drive communal vision. It is important to understand this, because cities are filled with well-meaning visionaries with great ideas who have a thinly veiled disdain for the businesses and business leaders of their community. They hold out the profit motive as some dirty little secret that taints every idea or interest on the part of the businessperson.

Unfortunately, this perspective greatly limits what can be accomplished within our communities. Having great communal ideas that ignore how local businesses might contribute to or even benefit from them is very much like trying to steer a car that has no engine. Some people may enjoy the quasi-prophetic role that this perspective allows them to play and may not require their ideas to be implemented. However, those who really want to contribute to the community have to swallow their pride and learn to work with local businesspeople.

The profit motive must be taken seriously as a limiting factor on what businesses can or cannot be expected to contribute, but it is certainly not a moral flaw for those who have to operate under its constraints. For instance, in our current economy, it usually makes more sense economically for most businesses to build buildings that have a thirty-year life span at best. These are not the kind of buildings that contribute to the local culture of a city. However, we cannot just expect an individual business to buck this trend and build a beautiful building at its own expense. This would drive up costs and therefore prices in a highly competitive environment, which could literally drive the owners out of business.

We need to be willing to shape our communal vision and then figure out how to realistically invite participation in this vision by our local businesses. In Missoula, a great example of this kind of partnership is the Missoula Redevelopment Agency (MRA). In the 1980s Missoula's downtown was in serious trouble. It was deemed an urban renewal district and was targeted for governmental support. The method of support involved harnessing tax revenue for the good of all downtown businesses. Property taxes were frozen at 1980 levels for city revenue.

As property values went up, the extra revenue went into a special fund for urban renewal that was managed by the MRA. The MRA used these funds to encourage and support local efforts that improved the downtown. Often these projects were initiated by local businesses, and the MRA both broadened the vision and provided the necessary capital. These projects ranged from the restoration of a downtown building to its original design and the inclusion of historic lampposts on a new bridge, to the construction of a hand-carved carousel in the middle of the downtown. Each of these projects made the downtown more interesting and charming, which helped bring customers to downtown businesses, which further increased property values and tax revenues.

There are all sorts of ways that businesses can help maintain the local culture of a place. But we must be realistic about their particular strengths (and their weaknesses) if we are going to see them fulfill this important role.

To say that we are from some place—be that Houston, Portland, or Memphis—is an important aspect of our identity—our identity before ourselves, before others, and before God. Unfortunately, not only is our population becoming increasingly transitory, making it difficult to develop a history with a place, more and more geographical locations are becoming standardized and losing any sense of place. We have traded in this idea of place by patronizing the chain retail stores, with their cheaper prices and a staggering variety of choices. And we are trying to fill a void—left by an absence of meaningful places to call our homes—with all of the stuff that is offered to us in the huge box stores on the edge of town.

To break this cycle, we cannot simply turn our backs on the economic and commercial features of our cities and try to pursue some ideal of voluntary simplicity on our own. Like Thoreau leaving Walden Pond to do his laundry in town, such individual attempts at rejecting commercialism often really only disguise the economic structures that support the utopian dream. Rather, we must acknowledge our dependence on the economic infrastructure for our day-to-day lives and then strive to make that infrastructure as enriching as possible.

9

Critical Mass
and Making Friends

The next sabbath almost the whole city gathered to hear the word of the Lord.

Acts 13:44

I found myself surprised to be appreciating the primal energy of adolescence, as I heard it identify more directly and vividly than adults ever would the variety of ways in which humans experience the need to gather in one place, which has always been, and still is, the reason for cities.

Daniel Kemmis, *The Good City and the Good Life*

■ A Carousel for Missoula

During the weekend I came out to Missoula to interview for my current position, my host took me to see the MCT production of *Carousel*. It was quite an impressive show. The eighty members of the cast were backed by a full symphony orchestra. The leads were professional-level, and the full-cast numbers were as good as anything I've seen on Broadway. Even the staging of the play was impressive—an elaborate backdrop descended from one-hundred-foot cavity above the stage, marking each scene change. This professional-level fly system, as well as the gilded and ornate interior, was part of seeing a show in the historic Wilma Theatre—built in 1921 and known as the "showplace of Montana."

Later that weekend, I learned the reason that MCT had chosen to perform *Carousel* at that particular time. A few years back, a Missoula resident named Chuck Kaparich had come up with a wonderful idea. He had seen a wooden carousel in Spokane and was inspired to create something like it in Missoula. After extensive research and a clumsy try at carving his first horse, Kaparich decided that it could be done. He brought his horse into the mayor's office and made a pitch. With the backing of the mayor and the Missoula Redevelopment Agency, the community started to get involved. Individuals and organizations could sponsor a horse by paying for the materials, by designing the horse, and by carving it.[1] Soon everyone from the elementary school kids to the Sons of Norway and the local newspaper was working on a horse.

Four days a week from 7:00 to 10:00 P.M., members of the community were in Kaparich's garage, working on the horses. Each horse was individually designed, and so dozens of people had to be trained in sketching, carving, and painting these majestic creations. The horses each took between four hundred to eight hundred hours to complete, and they were being completed on schedule. The mayor's office and the Missoula Redevelopment Agency were working to secure a space on the riverfront for the carousel. Soon a used frame and mechanical workings were refurbished, so the horses had a place to go. And Scott Olsen, who had some expertise in mechanical band organs, installed a glorious one at the carousel. On May 27, 1995, five years after Kaparich caught his vision, the Carousel for Missoula was opened to the public. And to help celebrate the event, MCT planned to open the show *Carousel* the same weekend.

All my life I had lived in large cities, and I didn't know how I would react to a place with just 65,000 inhabitants. I distinctly remember thinking during that weekend that Missoula is a city and not a small town. What led to this conclusion was the critical mass in Missoula that allowed one man's vision to be taken so far. In a more remote setting, Kaparich could have carved one horse or painted a picture of a carousel. In a small town, he could have developed a carousel consisting of prefab components. Only in a place with critical mass could he have created such a masterpiece as the Carousel for Missoula. And only in an exceptional city would there be a full-scale Broadway-quality musical performed in its honor.

■ Critical Mass

Critical mass, then, is the fifth marker of the city. The literal meaning of critical mass is "the smallest mass of fissionable material that will sustain a nuclear chain reaction at a constant level."[2] With regard to cities and their inhabitants, critical mass cannot be ascertained with such precision as it can in a laboratory. However, it is possible to describe some conditions that indicate its presence. Critical mass can be understood as the number and concentration of people required for friendships to be formed and coalitions to be built around a fairly narrow interest or specialization. It can also be understood as the number or concentration of people required to support a full-time artistic community or to provide a broad enough audience to hear new ideas. But, as with other aspects of city life, critical mass is most accurately perceived by intuition. As social creatures, we tend to be attracted to and comfortable in situations where critical mass is achieved.

There is an old adage from the youth ministry model developed by Young Life that you should choose a room for your youth group meeting that is slightly too small for the group that you expect to attend. That means if you are expecting only four students to come, you should meet in a phone booth. Kids feel safer and more willing to interact when they are comfortably crowded. Young Life has long understood the psychological and spiritual importance of critical mass to an effective ministry. Of course, people need space as well—and perhaps this is why Young Life also has a major emphasis in camping ministry. We need to create situations where people have space to be alone. However, over the past fifty years, we have overemphasized our need for space in this country, and we need to recover a sense of the use for and value of critical mass in our cities.

■ The City as Incubator, Gateway, and Patron

I have up until this point avoided defining a city on the basis of raw population numbers because critical mass is probably a better way to think about population requirements for cities. A very large population that is very spread out and not connected may not achieve a sense of critical mass. And a somewhat smaller population, like that of Missoula, may achieve critical mass rather easily because of its strong community networks. Critical mass is more important than raw population because it acts as an incubator for ideas and relationships, a gateway from which to disseminate ideas, and a support base for cultural activities.

The City as Incubator

Saint Augustine's mother prayed fervently that he would not go to Rome. She wanted him to become a Christian, and her concern was that this city would have a corrupting influence on her already rebellious son. What she didn't consider was the fact that among all of the various influences that he might encounter in the city of Rome, some of them might be for the good. God denied Monica her literal prayer but granted her the prayer of her heart. One night, Augustine sneaked onto a boat and headed off to Rome—an act that caused his mother unspeakable grief. But it was in Rome that Augustine received his invitation to teach in Milan (another great city), met his great spiritual mentor, Ambrose, and eventually became a Christian. As a result of this auspicious event, an important pillar of Western civilization was set in place.

◈

John Knox was fleeing persecution for his Protestant beliefs in his Scottish homeland. He came to Geneva looking for refuge and like-minded souls. It was there that he met John Calvin and was struck by his highly developed system of Reformed Protestant thought. Calvin became an important spiritual mentor for Knox. Under Calvin's influence, Knox developed a system of church government that became the foundation for the Presbyterian Church in Scotland. And the Presbyterian form of government in turn became a model for the emerging government in the United States.

◈

John Wesley was visiting London when he happened upon a meeting at Aldersgate Street. It was here, during a reading from Luther's preface to the book of Romans, that his heart was "strangely warmed." This heartfelt experience of the Christian faith gave Wesley a renewed passion for evangelism and led to a revival in England and around the world. Not only was the Methodist church formed out of his experience, but also a shift occurred away from dead orthodoxy toward an emphasis on a personal relationship with Christ. This rediscovery of the relational aspect of our faith would prove to be foundational for the evangelical community around the world.

◈

It is impossible to say what the church would look like today had it not been for the influential role that cities have had in its growth and development. It is easy, however, to point to any number of watershed events for the church that took place within cities. These major events represent only the smallest fraction of events that have been preserved in our history. We can assume countless other encounters that may have less global significance but have been equally significant on a personal level. The city as an incubator of ideas and friendships has been an invaluable asset to the Christian church throughout the centuries.

Certainly, it is not the church alone that has benefited from the critical mass of cities. Cities have played a key role in the development of civilization. The meeting of minds afforded by the city has facilitated great advancements in politics, science, and the arts. Insofar as Christians are invested in the advancement of truth and the development of culture, we can value cities for their role in bringing people together in this way.

Often, the encounters between kindred spirits in a city become formalized into a coalition or specialized interest group that then uses the natural flow of people and ideas in the city to perpetuate its cause. Missoula is filled with examples of such coalitions. Our community has provided a home base for more specialized interest groups per capita than any place I have lived before. We are the permanent home for the Boone and Crocket Club, the Rocky Mountain Elk Foundation, and the Center for the Rocky Mountain West. One of our newer additions is the Chalice of Repose, which focuses on the use of music in palliative care. Students are instructed in the use of harp music to help people make the transition into death with grace and beauty. We host the International Wildlife Film Festival every year, as well as an International Choral Festival every three years. Of course there are some more colorful gatherings on our yearly calendar, such as the Maggot Fest (a rugby tournament), and the Miss Con convention (for those interested in extraterrestrial life forms).

A college or university within a city represents a highly developed and formalized example of such coalition building. Not all cities have a significant university within their borders, and not all great universities are to be found in cities. However, a city that is the home to a great university has many distinct advantages. The university as a whole is a kind of loose coalition advocating the free exchange of ideas. And each academic department within the university is a specific coalition. Finally, because universities operate somewhat outside of the market economy, they bring to a city or town people who wouldn't normally have a reason or the means to be there. The university thus actually brings representatives from outside coalitions and cultures into a city, greatly enriching the mix of ideas.

Last summer, a woman in our college ministry felt a call to go on a short-term mission to Bosnia. We had found a mission organization to work out the logistics and to connect her to missionaries in Bosnia, but no one in our campus ministry personally knew much about Bosnia. The first meeting of the committee that we formed to help with her preparation betrayed our collective ignorance:

"Bosnia is in Eastern Europe, right?"
"Weren't we at war with Bosnia?"
"It's still called Bosnia, isn't it?"

Clearly, our ability to prepare this student for her mission was going to be limited. Fortunately, our enterprising student contacted the International Student Association and found six students at the university who were actually from Bosnia. Contacting these six students before her trip provided a much better orientation to Bosnian culture than we would have been able to do with hours of research.

One of the difficulties people sometimes have in living in a small town is the sense of suffocation and stifling conformity that can be endemic in the community. A university offsets such features of small-town life. The professors add an interesting voice to our public debates and voting trends. The students are active channels for national and world trends. And the lectures and conferences, though targeted to the university community, bring a caliber and variety of people, events, and ideas into our neighborhood that wouldn't otherwise be there.

The City as Gateway

Critical mass is particularly important to Christians because we have a mandate to "make disciples of all nations" (Matthew 28:19), and cities that are characterized by critical mass can be extremely useful in multiplying our efforts. Critical mass is probably the reason that the apostle Paul chose to focus his ministry on the cities of the Mediterranean world. The conversion of Lydia provides a good example:

We set sail from Troas and took a straight course to Samothrace, the following day to Neapolis, and from there to Philippi, which is a leading city of the district of Macedonia and a Roman colony. We remained in this city for some days. On the Sabbath day we went outside the gate by the river, where we supposed there was a place of prayer; and we sat down and spoke to the women who had gathered there. A certain woman named Lydia, a worshiper of God, was listening to us; she was from the city of Thyatira and a dealer in purple cloth. The Lord opened her heart to listen eagerly to what

133

was said by Paul. When she and her household were baptized, she urged us, saying, "If you have judged me to be faithful to the Lord, come and stay at my home." And she prevailed upon us.[3]

Paul met not only Jews and members of various philosophical schools in the cities, but residents of other cities and regions as well. We know from Revelation that Thyatira was one of the seven churches of Asia, but Paul never went to Thyatira to start a church there.[4] Most likely by meeting Lydia in Philippi, Paul was able to indirectly bring the gospel to this city in Asia. Paul chose cities as the focus of his ministry because cities are where new ideas can get a hearing and perhaps have an impact. For similar reasons, in this country evangelists such as Dwight Moody, Billy Graham, and Luis Palau have focused their efforts on the cities. And organizations such as Promise Keepers and Youth for Christ have focused much of their efforts on the cities.

The City as Patron

Critical mass can have value even outside of its benefit to our strategies for evangelism. As Christians, we have a stake in what goes on in our communities. As we examined in the last chapter, Paul has encouraged us to think about things that are excellent and "worthy of praise."[5] The formal arts certainly can fit that description. Art galleries, the theater, and the symphony enrich our lives and deepen our understanding of ourselves and the world around us.

But the formal arts can exist only when there is sufficient patronage for such things. You might find a summer stock theater or a few private galleries in a resort town, but it is only in cities that you will find a full symphony orchestra or a year-round theater group. There can be very fine examples of summer stock theater or summer concert series in all sorts of obscure locations. But these performances, by necessity, have to be of the tried-and-true variety to survive. It is the season subscribers at regular theater companies or symphonies who allow experimentation and development of the form. Without cities and their critical mass, we would most definitely see an impoverishment of the arts.

■ Allowing Critical Mass

Critical mass can be a great asset to a particular locale and in many respects is a sign of the health and prosperity of an area. If the job market is good, housing is available, and the quality of life is perceived to be good, an area will naturally increase its critical mass. On the other hand, without these basic ingredients, it can be very difficult to develop critical mass even if there is a great desire to do so.

However, there are policy-level issues that can have a great influence on critical mass, even in a prosperous and vibrant area. A city can unwittingly inhibit its potential for critical mass through ill-conceived policies and regulations. The two areas for which policies are commonly counterproductive have to do with density and connectivity. We will examine both of these issues in more detail.

Density

Density is an important concept for us to understand with regard to cities because it is frequently misunderstood. The word *density* in public discourse is almost universally used in a pejorative sense. Low-density housing situations are assumed to be the ideal for those who can afford them, whereas high density is assumed to be a necessary evil for those who have no other options. Density bonuses for new construction are assumed to be a conspiratorial strategy on the part of governments and developers to squeeze the maximum revenue from the smallest parcels of land.

What is seldom taken into consideration in these debates is that some of the most sought-after residences in this country are in high-density settings. Park Avenue in New York City and Nob Hill in San Francisco are two well-known examples. The reason for the confusion seems to be that people tend to confuse the terms *density* and *overcrowding*. According to Jane Jacobs:

> High densities mean large numbers of dwellings per acre of land. Overcrowding means too many people in a dwelling for the number of rooms it contains. The census definition of overcrowding is 1.5 persons per room or more. It has nothing to do with the number of dwellings on the land, just as in real life high densities have nothing to do with overcrowding.[6]

This is an important distinction for us to make, because what is needed for the healing of our cities is maximizing their critical mass by making them higher in density rather than lower. Sprawl is the inevitable result of a large number of people attempting to live near the services of the city in the lowest possible density. Using appropriate levels of high-density development within cities allows cities to function well and can preserve the outlying areas as wilderness or farmland.

Some planning tools that have been used to encourage this kind of development are density bonuses, growth rings, and infill. Density bonuses give tax advantages to developers who build at higher levels of concentration within city limits. Growth rings define urban boundaries somewhat rigidly—encouraging development within the boundary while restricting it outside of the boundary. Infill is a result of growth rings and simply means developing and improving sites within city limits before looking outside for development opportunities.

Of course, as with all policies and legislation, there are well-conceived examples and there are poor examples. Just because a municipality uses phrases like *growth ring* or *density bonus* in a proposed piece of legislation, this does not guarantee that it will provide a good example of the application of these concepts. In most cases, it requires an intimate knowledge of local conditions and a great deal of political acumen to write and enact legislation that encourages the healthy development of critical mass. However, very little will be accomplished in this area so long as words like *density* are misunderstood by the general public.

Connectivity

The other concept that requires some clarification with regard to critical mass is that of connectivity. Very often, even in medium- to high-density conditions, critical mass is not achieved because of a lack of connectivity. You may live in a housing subdivision that is only a hundred yards from a grocery store. However, if you ever try to walk that hundred yards to pick up something at the store, you will soon discover the importance of connectivity. Most likely you will find a fence or a drainage ditch between your housing subdivision and the store to which you are attempting to walk. Even if you manage to make your way past these physical barriers, when you reach the store, you will probably be greeted by the back of the store with no door through which to gain access. You will then have to walk all the way around the store to find the entrance.

This hundred-yard walk is a grueling and unsatisfying experience because no one is supposed to want to walk between the house and the store. What people are supposed to do is to get into their cars, drive through their subdivision onto the collector road, and make their way to the store through the major streets.

The idea of single-use zoning is so pervasive in our mindset that even when different kinds of uses happen to be adjacent to each other, they are required to be separated by some kind of physical barrier like a fence or a ditch. So long as these fences and ditches remain—separating our residences from our stores—people will rarely attempt to walk from one to the other. Even where no physical barrier exists, our cul-de-sac style of street design also impinges on the connectivity among houses in a particular subdivision. Such physical conditions mean not only that we will walk to the store much less frequently, but also that our chance of running into another human being on the way to the store is almost non-existent.

Whatever we may personally feel about the experience of walking versus driving, if our municipal laws or our street designs require that we drive our cars to the store, we will not have the opportunity to meet or greet anyone on the way. It would be well worth our time to find these separation requirements in our municipal codes, expose these assumptions that govern our suburban design, and work to have them removed.

Critical mass is an important but easily misunderstood feature of urban life. It has played a key role in much of the development of civilization and much of the progress for the kingdom of God. But it is destined for extinction in this country if we continue in our sprawling pattern of growth. In our attempts to avoid crowding and to preserve personal space, we have cut ourselves off from the rest of humanity and have severely limited the kinds of collective achievements that we can make as a species. Ultimately, collective humanity cannot solve every problem and create unlimited good. We must honestly acknowledge our limitations. However, the more we can preserve and create the quality of critical mass in our future development, the more we will see evidence of what humanity can achieve.

10

Strangers and Hospitality

You shall also love the stranger, for you were strangers in the land of Egypt.

Deuteronomy 10:19

The bedrock attribute of a successful city district is that a person must feel personally safe and secure on the street among all these strangers.

Jane Jacobs, *The Death and Life of Great American Cities*

■ Estranged in Suburbia

As I have mentioned earlier, my direct experience of suburbia has been limited to living in a suburb for one month following college. Admittedly, this was not nearly enough time to give a fair assessment of its problems and possibilities. However, it did give me the opportunity to see this kind of human environment through a particular lens. While I was living in this environment I was essentially a stranger and was able to experience suburbia as a stranger would. Of course, in the house in which I was living, I was a guest. But when I left the confines of that private house, I became a stranger.

I became aware of this reality during the course of a few days that I had taken off work for some rest and restoration. I had noticed during my commute that the surrounding countryside was beautiful and invited further exploration. So I decided on the next Friday to spend the day trying to get a better sense of the terrain. When Friday came, I grabbed my daypack, got in my car, and headed for the base of the highest peak in the area. As I got closer to where I thought that I wanted to embark, I realized that there was no clear place that I could park my car. The road came clear up to somebody's fence, and there wasn't a clear right-of-way for public use. Eventually, I decided to park the car to the side of what looked to be somebody's private driveway and I got out to look around.

What I found was a number of fences dividing the land among its various owners. Some of it might have been public land, but it was difficult to ascertain. There were a few houses in view within some of the open land. This gave the impression that at least some of the fences that I was thinking about crossing led into someone's front yard. I felt like an intruder and was worried that someone in one of the houses was watching my every move and was writing down the license number of my car, which was parked in their driveway. By that time, my sense of adventure was spoiled, and I got back into my car, drove up the hill as far as the public road would take me, and returned home less than an hour after I had left.

Now I'm reasonably sure that I was just a little paranoid in that situation. And if I had grown up in that area and had known Mr. Brown and Mrs. Jones personally, I would have felt perfectly free to cross the fences into their respective lands and explore around for a bit. And they probably would have no problem with me if I had done so. The point is that as a stranger, I lacked the personal relationships necessary to navigate that particular situation, and I lacked experience in that kind of setting to know what kind of behavior is permitted. What I read from the physical environment was the message that if you are not from here, you have no business being here. And so, estranged from this beautiful setting, I retreated to the private domain to which I had been given more explicit access. I realized on that day yet another feature of city life that I had taken for granted, never having lived in any other kind of setting. A city is a place where it is acceptable to be a stranger.

■ Welcoming Strangers and the Limits of Interpersonal Decisions

This final marker of city life is one that we might hesitate to call good but is significant nonetheless. Whatever we may feel about it personally, the inescapable fact is that cities are places where we encounter strangers. If cities sometimes help connect people who want to be con-nected, cities are also places people come to because they don't have any connections. In a small town everyone knows everyone, and the stranger stands out simply by not being known. In a suburb (as I came to discover), people in a particular vicinity may not know each other per-sonally, but because every aspect of life is so privatized, the stranger lit-erally has no place to stand, walk, or park a car.

In a city you come to expect that many people you will see through-out your day are going to be strangers. There is not, therefore, a stigma attached to being a stranger. Cities are among the few places where strangers are accepted, and consequently, people who have no signifi-cant network of people come to cities because they can.

This is significant for Christians, because the Bible holds hospitality—especially hospitality for strangers—in high regard. In the Old Testament, this was an important part of being God's people: "You shall also love the stranger, for you were strangers in the land of Egypt" (Deut. 10:19). In the New Testament, this mandate is given with even more force as Jesus teaches in the parable of the sheep and the goats:

> Then the king will say to those at his right hand, "Come, you that are blessed by my Father, inherit the kingdom prepared for you from the foundation of the world; for I was hungry and you gave me food, I was thirsty and you gave me something to drink, I was a stranger and you welcomed me, I was naked and you gave me clothing, I was sick and you took care of me, I was in prison and you visited me." Then the righteous will answer him, "Lord, when was it that we saw you hungry and gave you food, or thirsty and gave you something to drink? And when was it that we saw you a stranger and welcomed you, or naked and gave you clothing? And when was it that we saw you sick or in prison and visited you?" And the king will answer them, "Truly I tell you, just as you did it to one of the least of these who are mem-bers of my family, you did it to me."[1]

The possibility of meeting strangers, getting to know their stories, and possibly extending some kindness to them is an important opportunity for Christians who live and work in the city. I sometimes volunteer at our local food bank, and every time I am called to work, I am reminded in a tangible way that not all is well in Missoula. The food bank is the last resort to which people can turn once a month if their income falls short. A popular saying in this town is, "You can't eat the scenery"—at the food bank you realize how true this is. Here you read the poverty statistics for our region on the faces of those who require its services. A handful of the clients you might call stereotypical transients. But by and large, the clients are responsible, hardworking people (many with children) who have fallen on hard times.

I remember one woman in particular who looked like she could have been one of my parents' friends. She was well dressed and had the social confidence of someone who was more accustomed to being self-sufficient. It took all of her courage to show up at the food bank and ask for help. But things had started to unravel in her life, and her self-sufficiency had quite recently come to an end. Perhaps her husband had left her, or she had lost her job or had a medical emergency. I never asked. In any case, she wasn't ready to face her friends and was glad to be able to accept compassion as a stranger from strangers. Working at the food bank is a sobering experience, but it is also comforting in a way. I am reminded how fragile life is, as are all the security measures we prop up around ourselves. But I am also reminded that we know a God who cares for the stranger and who commands his people to have compassion for the stranger.

Many Christians are familiar with God's concern for the stranger and are committed in theory to the idea of showing compassion to this vulnerable population group. However, this commitment, if we are going to really take it seriously, should have implications not only for our interpersonal decisions—such as when we have to decide whether or not to strike up a conversation with a stranger or whether or not we should give spare change to someone who asks. But this commitment should have some bearing on our residential and vocational decisions as well. We may be individually ready to welcome strangers if we were to encounter them, but if we place ourselves solely in private spheres at home and at work, this will be all but impossible, and we will rarely, if ever, have to follow through on this commitment. Conversely, by choosing to live or work in cities, where strangers actually are to be found, we put ourselves in a position to be obedient to Christ's command concerning the stranger.

I realize that I am not the only person who has made this observation. And further, being the father of three young children, I would be among the first to admit that there are some significant problems involved in trying to put this into practice. The first is that what it means to welcome a stranger needs to be more carefully defined. As our children have become more independent, we have had to teach them appropriate ways to interact with strangers. As Kate and I walk to preschool, we have adopted the practice of greeting everyone that we meet on the way with a cheerful "Good morning." When we are waiting at the bus stop in the presence of others, we have encouraged our children to ask for and volunteer information concerning names, and ages (if it's another child), and to make light conversation.

On the other hand, we have been vigilant about teaching our children to be wary of strangers. "Do not take candy from a stranger" and "Do not get into a car with a stranger" are no longer middle-class clichés (as my friends and I used to treat them) but are important survival skills for our children. So when I suggest that we might make residential and vocational decisions that would put us and our families in greater contact with strangers, I do not mean to imply that we naively expose our private lives to those who might do us harm. Rather, I mean that we should put ourselves in situations where we encounter strangers so that we can practice the delicate social practice of welcoming strangers in appropriate and relatively safe ways.

A second and related point is that there is significant danger in many of the places where strangers gather in the greatest concentration. Gang activity, random violence, prostitution, and other social ills are to be found precisely in the places where we would encounter strangers. This is a problem with origins that run very deep in our culture and for which a viable solution is far beyond the scope of our interpersonal, residential, or vocational decisions. While there are some Christians who have responded nobly to the call to move their families into dangerous urban environments, I must admit at this point that I would not feel comfortable making this decision for my own family.

Nevertheless, there is a whole continuum of types of environments in which strangers will be present in a greater or lesser degree. So there is room for individuals and families to challenge themselves to go farther along this continuum. And there are strategies that we can employ, wherever we live, that might begin to heal a culture that has forgotten how to welcome the stranger.

■ Strangers as Indicator Species

The problem of strangers and the danger that they can bring to us and to our families is a significant one in our culture, and one to which we need to devote much discussion and energy to help find a solution. One place to begin this discussion is to ask "Who's problem is it?" Is it only a problem for those who are unfortunate enough to have no option but to live and try to raise a family in a dangerous area? Is it a problem for a government that may have failed to provide adequate social services or police protection to keep certain areas safe? Or is it a problem for all of us? My initial sense is that it is probably a problem that belongs to all of us.

What has led me to this conclusion has been the role of systems theory in my understanding of how families work. Anyone who has worked with young people for any length of time will have some experience with a "problem kid." This kid is a problem in the youth group and is a problem to the family as well. One way of dealing with this "problem kid" is to try to figure out what is wrong with him or her as an individual. What can we do or say to this person to fix this problem? Systems theory has taught us that often it is not the individual kid that is the problem, but that the kid is often the weakest link, through which the family's larger problems are made manifest. Any effective solution to this kind of a problem will have to involve the whole family if it is going to be effective.

Now, families often don't want to hear about this theory when the implication is that it is their family system that isn't working. Often they will try every kind of solution for the individual kid and even go so far as to cut off the "problem kid" from the rest of the family. If they refuse to consider the possibility that the problem is with the system, not only will they never see their "problem" fixed, but they are most likely going to see future problems in other vulnerable parts of the family system.

This systems approach has been applied usefully to the natural environment as well. When a vulnerable indicator species becomes endangered, we know that the entire ecosystem oftentimes is in danger. And we must look to solutions that heal the ecosystem rather than just try to save the species.

I see the same kind of situation facing us in our contemporary American culture. The stranger, as the most vulnerable member of our society, is our "problem kid," as it were, and we as a culture are trying to fix this problem in isolation. We deal with the danger and chaos found in areas with lots of strangers by targeting them for social services and police protection. At the same time, we cut ourselves off from strangers in our homogenized suburban environments and our gated communities. What we are discovering, however, is that this individualized approach is not working. The problems caused by strangers in the city are not going away, and at the same time we are beginning to see more and more examples of violent behavior popping up in other weak links within the sanitized and "safe" world of our suburbs.

This may be an appropriate time, then, to ask the question of where the system has broken down. What systemic problems are made manifest in the mess that we have made of many of our urban cores? And what positive attributes of human interaction have we lost by spending the last half-century isolating ourselves from one another? It is to these questions that we now turn.

Civility

Civility can be defined as "the formal politeness that results from observing social conventions."[2] The rules governing these social conventions emerge quite naturally within contexts that require people to interact with one another. There are always going to be acts of incivility and even uncivil people, but there will also be formal and informal censures for such behavior and such people, so as to keep these manifestations of the concept the exception rather than the rule.

One of the consequences of our automobile-oriented culture has been a significant reduction in the amount of personal contact that we have with one another. Almost every moment we spend driving a car alone is time that would otherwise have been spent in the company of another person. And this reduction in time spent with other people has greatly reduced the civility that we exhibit toward one another. Not only have we gotten out of practice with regard to civil behavior toward one another, we have learned patterns of interaction that are decidedly uncivil. The way that we curse and gesture to fellow motorists while driving our cars is nothing short of barbarism. We see the fruits of this incivility in our shock radio programs, TV talk shows, and Internet discussions.

Since many of our social conventions governing civil behavior have to do with appropriate ways to interact with strangers, it should come as no surprise that strangers have borne the brunt of our uncivil culture. Perpetual strangers have often been degraded by the cumulative effect of day-in-day-out incivility. And many of these same strangers have learned a kind of incivility as a defense mechanism against a hostile public. Therefore, while it may seem a laughably small place to start, one place to begin increasing the safety of our cities may be in the simple act of relearning the practice of civility.

There will always be strangers among us, and we may never open our homes or our lives up to them completely, but we can reduce their strangeness to us and our strangeness to them by engaging them in light conversation. As was mentioned above, this is something that I am trying to demonstrate to my children as we walk around the neighborhood or wait at the bus stop. Those who don't live in an area where one can easily encounter strangers for this purpose can look for other occasions to practice this skill. Going to the mall, a sporting event, or a community festival can provide occasions for us to be intentional about developing this skill and teaching it to our children.

The practice of being civil toward one another and looking for occasions that lend themselves to such behavior can help to make us more humane as individuals, but it can also increase our safety in some very real and tangible ways. Some friends of mine were in Paris when the attack on the World Trade Center occurred. Theirs was among the first flights to leave Paris for the United States, and understandably, everyone was a bit nervous about their safety. Before the flight, the pilot got on the intercom to try to reassure everybody. After explaining how thoroughly everybody and everything had been checked, he then asked the passengers to take a moment to introduce themselves to the people who were seated next to them. My friends reported that they felt a great sense of relief after this exercise.

My first thought, upon hearing this story, was that the pilot did this to increase the likelihood of identifying any potential terrorists by using the collective instincts of the passengers. But then, I began to think that (whatever his motivations were) there may have been another, more profound effect of this exercise. Perhaps a more important outcome was that by responding to this simple request for civility, a potential terrorist may have learned the name and story of one of his or her potential victims. To commit an act of mass destruction of civilians, a person usually needs to generalize and demonize the enemy. The less they can be thought of as humans with hopes and fears similar to one's own, the easier it is to rationalize the termination of their lives. If a potential terrorist discovers that the person in the next seat is not only a capitalist infidel, but is also named Mark and has three young children named Nells, Luke, and Toren waiting for him at home, it may be that much harder to carry out a terrorist plan.

This strategy of getting to know strangers can be helpful to mitigate danger in such transitory situations, but it is even more effective in the places where we work and live. In Berkeley, some of the local churches pooled their resources and hired a pastor for the transients of the community. This woman worked day in and day out on the streets of Berkeley, getting to know these people's names and their stories. She was once asked whether she felt safe in her work. And she replied, "Sometimes I feel like the safest person in Berkeley." Most people in Berkeley feel a bit nervous when they encounter a transient in a back street or an alley, but this pastor knows just about all of them. Most of the transients consider her a friend, wouldn't dream of hurting her, and, further, would quickly come to her aid if needed. And of the ones who truly are dangerous, she is acutely aware of the real danger these individuals represent and knows how to take the necessary precautions.

Now, if you live or work in an area with a significant transient population, getting to know every homeless person in your community might not be a realistic goal. But you can practice civility by greeting the people that you meet with a friendly "hello" and learning the names of those people that you see on a regular basis. You can also look for an institution like a food bank or homeless shelter near your residence or place of work in which you can volunteer your time. Learning to be civil in that kind of controlled setting can expose you to some of the names and stories of the strangers in your community and can do a great deal for lessening your anxiety when you encounter them in other contexts.

145

Neighborliness

Another way to mitigate our fear of the stranger is to recover the practice of neighborliness. By getting to know our neighbors and being conscious of our role as neighbor, we lessen the territory in which we are vulnerable to the potential danger posed by the stranger. Neighborhoods where neighbors know each other and talk regularly are much less vulnerable to crime and violence than ones where neighbors are essentially strangers to one another. On our block everybody knows everybody else, and we are comforted by the fact that while we are away from the house or on vacation, our neighbors are watching our house for us. We also share information with one another about crime or suspicious behavior going on in our neighborhood. And while we have never experienced any kind of violence committed against any of the residents on our block, I cannot imagine any one of our neighbors not offering any help that would be needed if such a situation were to come about.

At first this might not seem like a very noble endeavor. It doesn't seem that much different from the "circle the wagons" approach of the gated community. But there are some distinct differences between these two strategies. In the first place, a nongated neighborhood does not restrict passage to the residents of that community. A stranger is perfectly free to walk through or even stop for a while in the public spaces of the neighborhood. The residents of a neighborhood are free to practice civility toward the stranger who enters their neighborhood; what neighborliness adds to the equation is a communal aspect of civility.

When I am deeply concerned that a stranger could terrorize my home and family, I will tend to be on my guard and defensive toward this potential intruder. But if I know that I am surrounded by a whole community that would come to my aid if a situation were to arise, I am more free to take the social risk of engaging the stranger in conversation and being civil toward him or her.

The virtue of neighborliness is not only something that I want for my neighborhood, but is something that I want deeply for every residential area. I can practice neighborliness in my context while advocating for a return to neighborliness in every context. We will discuss strategies for this in the next section. It is a bit optimistic, but not completely unrealistic, to say that if we increase the chance that the stranger in my neighborhood was raised among neighborly people in another real neighborhood, the chance of him or her engaging in antisocial behavior in my neighborhood is reduced.

Inherent Worth

Lastly, we need to deal with the issue of inherent worth. We are as a culture driven strongly by market forces. This not only has implications for our patterns of consumption and production, it also influences the worth that we assign to fellow human beings. There is a certain value that we assign to a person because of the market share that the person represents. And there is a certain value that we assign to a person because of the productive output for which he or she is responsible. Because of such valuations, there are two demographic categories of persons who have become strangers in our midst because they register on only one of these evaluative criteria.

The young people and the elderly in our society continue to be significant market forces in our economy because of the disposable income that they represent. But because they produce very little, they are not fully integrated into our civic life. As we have already observed, young people are relegated to one another's suburban basements, and elderly people are exiled in retirement communities. Neither of these groups participates in meaningful ways in our public life, to both our culture's impoverishment and their own.

By making "nonproductive" elderly people virtual strangers to the rest of our culture, we cut ourselves off from a huge population of potential role models for our children. And by making our young people completely dependent on their parents for access to our economic and cultural amenities, we deprive them of any venue for practicing interdependent public behavior.

As inexplicable as our recent spate of violence in the schools has been, one common theme has been the difficulty that the perpetrators had distinguishing fantasy from reality. I can't think of a more grounding experience for a young person than talking to an elderly person about his or her experience in a war or the Depression. But sadly, we have structured our everyday life so as to make such kinds of encounters increasingly rare. And furthermore, as the African-American community in this country has demonstrated, it is the grandmothers who have provided much of the social stability that remains in our inner-city neighborhoods. By forcing these gray-haired sentinels to the nursing homes, we give ourselves one more reason to fear the stranger.

To bring young people and the elderly into our public life, we will have to begin to see the noneconomic value that they provide for our culture. We will have to start valuing them as fellow humans regardless of the productive contribution that they make to our economy. By doing this, we will not only begin to integrate these forgotten groups into our culture to its betterment, we may even begin to assign more dignity and value to

147

the homeless stranger who also suffers the fate of the nonproducing member of our society.

■ The Twenty-Four-Hour City, Gentrification, and LULUs

Now, beyond the more subtle techniques of learning civility, neigh-borliness, and inherent worth, there are some policy-level strategies that we can employ to increase safety and create conditions under which our strangers are treated hospitably. One such strategy is to return to the idea of twenty-four-hour cities.

For the second half of the twentieth century, we convinced ourselves as a society that we could live in the suburbs and work and shop in the cities. What we discovered as we experimented with this flawed notion is that our cities became increasingly inhospitable for even the reduced functions that we had assigned to them. One of the most inhospitable elements of these specialized cities was the element of danger in them. We found further that we couldn't seem to reduce this danger significantly by increasing the police presence in these areas.

In the last few decades, we have come to rediscover the notion that no amount of police presence can take the place of a resident population invested in the cities in which they live. Jane Jacobs was among the first to rediscover this truth and has coined the phrase "eyes on the street" as an important way to understand this principle:

> There must be eyes upon the street, eyes belonging to those we might call the natural proprietors of the street. The buildings on a street equipped to handle strangers and to insure the safety of both residents and strangers, must be oriented to the street. They cannot turn their backs or blank sides on it and leave it blind. . . . The sidewalk must have users on it fairly continuously, both to add to the number of effective eyes on the street and to induce the people in buildings along the street to watch the sidewalks in sufficient numbers. Nobody enjoys sitting on a stoop or looking out a window at an empty street. Almost nobody does such a thing. Large numbers of people entertain themselves, off and on, by watching street activity.[3]

This notion has been rediscovered in recent years, and the cities that have been able to create the requisite conditions for "eyes on the street" are being called twenty-four-hour cities. They are enjoying the reputation of being safe places to live as well as interesting to visit, due to all of the activity. And as this favorable reputation leads more people and busi-

148

nesses to move to these cities, their desirability increases all the more. Twenty-four-hour cities are being recommended by major consulting firms as good places to invest, and cities that do not enjoy this designation are scrambling to figure out how they can achieve it.

One good example of a twenty-four-hour city is Vancouver, British Columbia. From a distance, it looks like a typical city with a skyline filled with high-rise buildings. However, what makes Vancouver different from many other cities is that the majority of the high-rise buildings are not office buildings but residential condominiums. A professor at Regent College who had recently moved to Vancouver explained to me that unlike in any other place he'd lived before, in Vancouver he allowed his teenage daughters to go downtown at night by themselves. There were always so many people walking around at any time of the day or night that he felt that they were reasonably safe.

One aspect of the twenty-four-hour city has to do with design and zoning. Every area of our city must have a sufficient number of residential units to create "eyes on the street," and each area must have a sufficient variety of commercial establishments to keep a steady flow of people on the street for those eyes to want to look at. Also, buildings must be designed in a way that encourages people to hang out at the street level and to observe activity on the street. And there must be clear markers of public and private space, so that order is easily preserved.

However, this concept of the twenty-four-hour city (and the more interesting and vibrant city life that it promotes) does lead into the sociological and demographic phenomenon known as gentrification. The issue of gentrification is somewhat controversial within New Urbanist discussions. We shall turn to these issues now.

Many of our cities are neglected and in great disrepair. However, they continue to be home for many members of our society and a source of low-cost housing for the people at the bottom of our socioeconomic ladder. When people in a higher socioeconomic class "rediscover" a city, they move in and begin to revitalize the region, thus creating more of a twenty-four-hour city. This leads to even more interest in moving to the region, and real estate prices begin to escalate. This first hits the renters, who are forced out of the area by rising rents. And, in time, it can hit the homeowners, as they see their property taxes go through the roof. What therefore can happen is that an area in the city is revitalized, but all of its original residents have to move out.

It must be observed that when living in an urban area is deemed an acceptable risk, such dramatic increases in property values occur because we have not provided nearly enough urban housing options over the past fifty years. As we rediscover the value of urban living, we should see more of this kind of real estate becoming available, and the dramatic effects on the market should calm down. In the meantime there are some strategies that can be employed to protect the interests of those who may be vulnerable to losing their homes. If the city is committed to the idea of a truly mixed-income area, there are mechanisms available that can make this a reality.

While gentrification is a sensitive issue (and needs to be watched for its most insidious effects), when we consider the alternatives, it really seems to be the best option for our cities. Not only does gentrification improve the residential and commercial appeal of an area, it brings in vital tax dollars, which can improve the schools and infrastructure of inner cities. I would even go so far as to say that governments and developers should encourage gentrification by better understanding how it happens.

According to experts, gentrification typically happens in three stages.[4] First the risk-oblivious people "discover" an area. These are young post-college-age people and artists. They tend to rent apartments and perhaps convert lofts into funky studios. Next come the risk-aware people, typically young professionals with some vision who are in a position to purchase properties. To secure bank loans, they have to update buildings to meet code and begin to improve the physical form of the area. Finally come the risk-averse people, who are preceded by developers who make significant financial investments in an area. It is at this stage that the real estate in the area becomes really expensive.

It's important that developers and city governments understand these stages so that they don't encourage the wrong kind of development at the wrong time. To go into an area of the city that is dilapidated and attempt to develop luxury condominiums is bound to end up as a failure. It is better, at this early stage, to make zoning and building codes flexible enough to allow the students and artists to create their own niche within the neighborhood. There may be a time when luxury condominiums would work in such an area, but the timing has to be right.

Finally, the other side of the gentrification debate has to do with the general question of how we are going to deal with poverty in our midst. We tend to associate poverty with crime and other antisocial behavior. But as the police chief of Charleston, South Carolina, observes "Urban problems are caused not by poverty, but by its concentration."[5] It is when a certain percentage of the population in an area is poor that we begin to see problems. This not only supports the need for at least some gentrification, but it also requires us to rethink our assumptions about low-income housing.

Our policy with regard to low-income housing has been to lump it all together in one limited geographical area. Perhaps we thought that we would limit its negative effects by restricting its physical space. This policy has been an abject failure and fortunately is no longer the reigning orthodoxy. Our more recent public housing projects tend to be much smaller and more scattered throughout the community. They are more scattered but not yet completely spread throughout our residential areas.

We have not yet seen very many low-income housing projects going into wealthy areas. Andres Duany, Elizabeth Plater-Zyberk, and Jeff Speck suggest that the only really workable solution to the potential problem of low-income housing is for every area to accept its fair share of what they call LULUs (Locally Undesirable Land Uses).[6] One of the main LULUs in our society will have to be low-income housing.

This is a position that will not be readily accepted by everybody—especially those residents of our wealthier neighborhoods. However, as Christians, this may be an area we want to adopt as one of our justice concerns and into which we should invest some of our moral clout. It is probably—in addition to being the right thing to do—the smartest thing for us to do as a culture. If the stranger is the weak link that is simply manifesting some of the systemic flaws in our culture, then we need to deal with this problem by bringing a few of the strangers back into our midst. We can continue to push them away and treat them as if they are the problem, but I don't think we will find this strategy to be very effective, either in preserving our safety or in enriching our culture.

■ The Good Urbanite

I realize that encouraging such nostalgic concepts as neighborliness, civility, and inherent worth seems a little weak against such pressing problems as guns, drugs, and gang activity in our cities. However, we must remember that Jesus' most clear teaching regarding our mandate toward the stranger came in response to the question of "who is my neighbor." So, with this in mind, I will end this section with an attempt to retell the parable of the good Samaritan in a more contemporary context.

There once was a man who was driving his beat-up Toyota Corolla from the city of Jericho to the city of Jerusalem. His car broke down and he didn't have a cell phone, so he had to walk to the next gas station. Because he was in a low-density area and there were no residents around to provide the necessary "eyes on the street" for safety, a band of latch-key suburban preadolescents attacked him (just like they had learned in the video game Street Fighter II) and left him for dead on the road.

First, a commuter from a nearby suburb drove by in his Jeep Cherokee. But since he was traveling so fast and his eyes were focused on the garish signs of the box stores on the fringes of Jerusalem, he could not notice anything so small as a human being on the side of the road. Next, a young person passed by in a Chevy Suburban. She actually noticed the distressed condition of this man and wanted to help. But since she was being driven to soccer practice by her dad (who was talking on his cell phone), and since she had never interacted with a stranger in a public setting, she didn't really feel as if she could do anything about the situation.

But then a pedestrian transient, who was engaged in the shameless act of walking on this public road, literally stumbled across the wounded man. He helped him get to the bus station, paid his fare, and took him to the Motel 6 adjacent to the Greyhound station. The pedestrian paid for his room and went to the 7-Eleven to buy aspirin and bandages (the nearest Now Care was fifteen miles away at another strip mall and impossible to get to on foot). Since there was no innkeeper to speak of, the pedestrian stayed with this man and nursed him back to health with alternating meals at McDonald's, Subway, and Taco John's.

And who do you think acted as a neighbor to the man who was in distress?

Conclusion: Seeking the Welfare of Your City

Your ancient ruins shall be rebuilt; you shall raise up the foundations of many generations; you shall be called the repairer of the breach, the restorer of streets to live in.

Isaiah 58:12

■ Lucrative Idealism

On the gulf coast of Florida near Panama City sits a little community known as Seaside. It is the prototype New Urbanist community, and the best-known example. Begun in 1981 by some of the pioneers of the New Urbanist movement, it was meant to demonstrate that the movement's principles could work when put into practice. In getting started, Seaside had the advantage of being a significant tract of land that was privately owned. There was no municipal government that had jurisdiction over Seaside, so its developers could write their own zoning codes.

In Seaside the best locations have been reserved for the public spaces—which are arranged into a harmonious and coherent layout. The private residences have been allowed to fill in around the public spaces. Each house in Seaside is individually designed and built, and no one architect has been allowed to design more than a few of the houses. Each house is distinct, but not one has a garage dominating the frontage. Every house has a welcoming front door as well as a front porch that is close enough to the street to facilitate casual conversations between home and street. There is a clear center to the town as well as a distinct edge, and it is about a five-minute walk from one to the other. The commercial hub is

153

in the center of town, but there is a good mix of uses and residential types throughout the community. The streets are comfortable for walking because of a good sense of enclosure. And the major streets terminate with some kind of an interesting view.

In short, Seaside breaks every rule in most municipal zoning codes and blatantly ignores the reigning orthodoxy among most commercial developers, both then and now. But has it worked? Have the lofty and erudite theories of New Urbanism held up to the brutal realities of the free market? So far, they seem to have done just that. Whereas property values for the rest of that region have been fairly stagnant, they increased ten-fold during Seaside's first ten years of existence. There was only one lot available for development at Seaside at the time of this writing. It has about a forty-five-foot frontage, and it is not an ocean-front lot. The current asking price is $2 million. If the market gives any indication of the tastes and preferences of the American population, then New Urbanism seems to have hit some kind of a nerve.

Fortunately, in the wake of Seaside's success, there are more New Urbanist developments being built all around the country. Over four hundred developments have been completed or are in process that have followed the New Urbanists' guidelines for Traditional Neighborhood Design (TND). And with each successful project, the next one becomes that much easier to finance and secure approval for. Municipal governments are becoming aware of the wisdom in the approach of the New Urbanists and are more and more willing to make exceptions in their zoning laws to allow for their kind of projects. Some cities are even rewriting some of their laws on the basis of New Urbanist principles. The city of Portland has enacted legislation in favor of narrow streets and against garage-dominated house fronts. And there are many other cities enacting similar legislation. The state of Wisconsin has even gone so far as to require all communities of more than 12,000 residents to adopt TND guidelines.

These trends not only apply to new developments, but are also being seen in traditional neighborhoods in historic cities and towns. People are rediscovering existing areas—which already have most of the TND elements—and are interested in living in such places. The renewed interest in urban amenities is driving up property values in some neighborhoods, but it is also leading to new investment in dilapidated areas. We are beginning to see a reversal in the trend of the past fifty years of continually pushing our homes and businesses to the fringes of our cities. People are moving back to the cities because they want to know their neighbors and they want to be able to walk to a coffee shop and they are willing to put up with some costs and inconveniences to do so.

As Christians, we can be encouraged by these trends. The real estate market now seems to be moving in a direction that better reflects some of our values—such as the importance of quality and intergenerational relationships. And our culture is embracing patterns of living that will enhance our effectiveness in ministry through increased opportunities for incarnational ministry and public discourse. Most of the time we find ourselves being called to swim against the tide of our dominant culture because of our faith commitments. But in the case of the New Urbanist movement and a renewed interest in historic cities and traditional neighborhoods, we can jump on board with enthusiasm. Insofar as we find these developments encouraging, we can participate in the New Urbanist movement in a number of ways.

The first and most fundamental thing that we can do is to simply be grateful for our cities and traditional neighborhoods. One thing that can be difficult about searching for practical applications for a "rediscovery of the city" is that one of our discoveries is that great cities can only be developed over many generations. We can't, through the exertion of our individual or collective will, just build a great city. Fortunately, we live in a country where the efforts of many generations have given shape to beautiful buildings and magnificent cities. We can begin by noting these examples and appreciating their grandeur.

In most cases this will involve walking more and driving less. We can learn to notice and appreciate the architectural beauty of the buildings and public spaces of our communities by walking around. This is a practice that I have learned from nature lovers and ecotourists. I know people in Montana who love a particular stretch of wilderness and know intimately every species of flora and fauna and the changes brought about by each season in that place. And I know people who will travel great distances to discover some new wonder of the natural world. After seven years of walking the streets of Missoula, I am beginning to understand a kind of intimate knowledge of a particular human environment. I also continue to see surprising and beautiful things even in my own neighborhood. And when I travel, I love to be surprised by fresh examples of urban beauty in other settings. The more we notice the urban beauty around us, the more we will work to preserve and support it.

The second thing that we can do is enjoy the cultural amenities of our cities. The arts used to thrive because there were wealthy patrons who decided to devote some of their financial resources toward various artistic endeavors. As we have already observed, that idea has been democratized in our current culture, and all of us are now, collectively, patrons for the arts. We can learn to take this role seriously in the city. A local theater needs season subscribers to really thrive in a community. Not only do these people provide the economic boost to get a season off to a good start, they also provide a base level of support to try out new shows and ideas. Each artistic venue in a community needs its faithful supporters. By choosing one area of interest and really getting behind it, you not only can enrich your life, you can support the richness of your community.

A third strategy for participating in the New Urbanist success has to do with your habits as a consumer. An awareness of New Urbanism can affect your strategy for homeownership. Potential homeowners typically have a set of standard questions that they ask of a real estate professional about a potential home. They want to know about square footage, about numbers of bedrooms and bathrooms, and (if they have children) about schools in the area. The real estate professional knows that a particular room needs to have a closet and an egress window to be considered a bedroom. It's not too hard to imagine a scenario where the potential homeowner asks whether or not a particular home is in a neighborhood. And, in time, the real estate professional will come to know that a neighborhood (as opposed to a subdivision) has a precise definition. It is a place with well-conceived and accessible public spaces, that is mixed-use in its zoning and is a five-minute walk from center to edge. As potential homeowners continue to ask about neighborhoods, we will see the market moving that much more quickly to provide these kinds of settings.

New Urbanism can affect our smaller-scale shopping patterns as well. We've already noted the advantages to our communities when local businesses thrive. We can support these businesses by forgoing the large chain retailers and shopping locally whenever possible. When we do this, we will not only support local culture and identity, but we will find our shopping to have a much more relational and fulfilling dimension. It may cost us a bit more to do this, but if we consider some of the junk that we spend our money on (and the stuff in our ministorage units), I think that we will find the trade-off to be negligible.

Last, some might find vocational implications of the New Urbanism. I think that this would be an exciting time to be a Christian architect, builder, or city planner. For most of the last century, these professions had been largely bureaucratized and lacking in a human dimension. The New Urbanism is bringing about a renewed public accountability to these professions. More and more communities are bringing together ordinary citizens and design professionals for day-long or week-long meetings to engage in joint planning for a particular area. These meetings, known as charrettes, have become an important planning tool in many municipalities. Through charrettes and other emerging practices, we are seeing a new openness to bringing issues of meaning and value into the public arena. Having Christians who are experts in their field at the forefront of these discussions could have a significant impact.

There is much to be encouraged about in the economic success of the New Urbanist movement and much that we can do to participate in its success. It is exciting to see the market and our culture moving in directions that we can affirm. But surely we will not always be able to take our cues directly from the current state of the market. And we cannot understand our contribution to this movement strictly from a consumer perspective. There remain three questions that might determine, or at least shape, our involvement in this movement as it unfolds before us. First, to what extent is the New Urbanism a novelty or a passing fad? Second, is the New Urbanism essentially an elitist movement? Finally, does the church have anything distinct to contribute to New Urbanism as a cultural phenomenon? We will take each of these questions in turn.

■ "New Urban" Revolution or Reformation?

There was a song that came out when I was in college, entitled "You Can't Fool the Children of the Revolution." In many ways the lyrics of this song helped to explain my emerging cynicism about cultural change. I had gone to UC Berkeley for college, partially because I was restless with what I perceived as the dominant middle-class culture. And I wanted to see what the counterculture had to offer. My first impression was that it was a more open, free, and engaging culture than the one to which I had already been exposed.

What I discovered over time came as quite a shock. In Berkeley, the counterculture had, in fact, become the dominant culture. And this particular "Berkeley culture" was no more open, free, or engaging than the one it had replaced. If your hair was too short or if you didn't have the proper Guatemalan attire, you were relegated to marginal status and couldn't participate fully in its traditions. Radical ideas had gained orthodox status, and there was a form of social censure for ideas that were deemed too conservative. My years at Berkeley taught me, if nothing else, that the world is a complex place.

The lesson behind most revolutionary movements throughout history is that what is new is often not much of an improvement on what has gone before. And so we find many people skeptical, as I had become, of new programs that are supposed to lead us toward problem-free utopias. This can lead to an interesting, and all-too-common, dilemma for many people. One can remain somewhat critical of the dominant culture, but at the same time not be ready to fully embrace the counterculture. This is exactly where five years of college had left me.

It is this perspective that has actually led me to an appreciation of the New Urbanist movement. What I value most about the New Urbanism is that there is nothing particularly *new* about it. You could say that Seaside represents a radical new direction in city planning, or you could say that Seaside represents a return to the way that virtually all towns were built in this country prior to 1945, and both statements would be accurate. I am confident that the New Urbanist movement is not calling us to a new and untried way of living together. If anything, the New Urbanists are challenging us to call the suburban experiment (that we have been conducting for the past fifty years) a failure and to get back to how we used to do things.

The track record for good urban design goes back quite a bit farther than just our experience in the United States would suggest. I am writing this final chapter from the Old Town section of Geneva, Switzerland. As I write I hear the hum of conversations going on at the corner café, I hear church bells just down the street and the steady sound of footsteps and laughter as people converse and greet each other as they make their way up and down these cobblestone streets to their houses or apartments. In many ways Geneva, though fairly small, is one of the most modern cities in the world. But for almost five hundred years, Geneva has steadily maintained the requisite conditions of vibrant urban life. And I am quite sure that very few people in this city have ever heard of the New Urbanist movement and that if I tried to explain it to them, they would certainly question my use of the word *new*.

Geneva as a model urban environment provides a good jumping-off place for two observations about the long history of urban life represented here. The first is that Geneva had been a city for many years, but it became a great city because of a Christian vision for the place. Martin Ferel, John Calvin, and Theodore Beza wanted to create an ideal Christian community here, and that vision took the distinct shape of a great city. Seeing this model inspired many people around the world with a renewed vision for their own cities. Roger Williams (the founder of Providence, Rhode Island) was among those who had been thus inspired by Geneva and who brought this vision to America. Most of the cities and towns from which the New Urbanists have received their inspiration were founded on similar Christian vision. Perhaps as the New Urbanists learn from and master the physical design of these inspired cities, there will be a new openness to the vision that lay behind these design decisions.

The second point that needs to be made concerning Geneva is that it is possible for a church to be in the center of a vibrant city and yet be on the margins of that city's culture. I attended two worship services this morning at the most central and well-known churches in the city, and there were fewer then two hundred in both services taken together. There were actually very vibrant and warm communities of faith at these two churches. However, even in this relatively small city of 200,000 residents, I wouldn't call either of these churches a major cultural force. Christian vision gave Geneva a strong foundation, but it no longer exercises a major influence on day-to-day life in this great city. And compared to the rest of the cities of Europe, Geneva may be on the more faithful end of the spectrum.

Unlike America, Europe has managed to preserve and develop its urban traditions into the present age. As a result, it has some of the most interesting and vibrant cities in the world. However, it is in Europe that we have seen the church experience the most radical decline in influence over the past century or so. This fact should remind us that even the best-designed and most charming cities will not automatically support the aims of the kingdom of God. The church cannot, and never could, rely on external forms of either ecclesial or civic institutions to guarantee the success of its mission. We need to be constantly reminded by the private Christians that our fundamental task continues to be evangelism of individuals through direct relationships. Despite my deep affection for urban charm, I have to concede that I would rather have tract homes and strip malls where the gospel is being openly shared and received than even the most engaging urban setting where it is not.

We do have some interesting opportunities for evangelism as a result of this renewed interest in urbanism in our country. Europe has its own historical reasons for the decline in Christian influence over the centuries. And its story does not need to be our story. We have an important mandate for mission developing alongside the New Urbanist movement. Most of the time mission work involves going out somewhere in order to bring the gospel to an unreached people. But in the case of our cities, our churches are already there. We don't have to "go out" to the cities. We simply have to be prepared for the people who are returning to us. As the trickle of people who are rediscovering the value of the city becomes a flood, the church will have an unprecedented ministry opportunity. I foresee some very interesting developments in urban ministry in this country over the next few decades.

■ Making the World Safe for Picket Fences

Another issue that needs to be settled with regard to the New Urbanism is to what extent it can be considered an elitist movement. This is an issue with which I wrestle on a personal basis. The historic University Neighborhood of Missoula is a coveted and expensive place to live. I feel very fortunate to be able to afford a home in this neighborhood, but I realize that this is not an option for most of the residents of Missoula. I sometimes wonder to what extent my interest in New Urbanism is simply an

159

attempt to justify and protect this charming and agreeable setting in which I find myself.

If New Urbanism is simply by elites and for elites, then it is not a cause worth fighting for, and it may even be morally questionable to participate in its ends. And it is certainly easy to come to the conclusion that it is in fact an elitist movement. To purchase a home in a well-preserved historic neighborhood or in a TND development is more expensive than buying a home in a typical suburban tract development. And buying a home in Seaside is an option only for the ultra-rich. Many of the issues that New Urbanists bring into the public debate (like beauty, quality, and charm) seem to be luxuries with which only the wealthy can afford to concern themselves. A common jibe among critics of the New Urbanist movement is that it is really about "making the world safe for picket fences."

There are a couple of points that need to be made in order to temper some extreme perspectives on this issue. The first is that ultimately, mixed-use zoning provides a greater range of options for all income classes. It is more expensive to buy a home in a historic neighborhood or in a TND, but it is also true that one can rent an apartment in one of these areas and have access to all of its amenities for quite a bit less. Second, by encouraging density and mixed-use zoning, New Urbanism makes walking and the use of public transportation much more viable options for most people. An average car costs about $6,000 per year to own and operate. If living in a urban environment can reduce a family's needs from three cars to one, their buying power for a home is greatly enhanced and may even make up for the difference in housing costs.

Finally, living in a quality urban environment is expensive because the market has been artificially restricted by zoning laws or has not yet adjusted to consumer preference. If supporting New Urbanism means working to increase the availability of housing in quality urban environments, then such work can only help to bring the prices of this kind of housing to a more affordable level. The fact of the matter is that New Urbanist principles for development and preservation are much more economical from a societal perspective than is the suburban model.

Two summers ago we took our youth group to Tijuana, Mexico, to build houses for some families in that area. We were on the outskirts of Tijuana, in a region that was considered to be among the worst of its slums. The area seemed to have been completely overlooked in terms of government institutions and services. It was in fact the lax zoning laws that allowed a group of high school students to build (and wire) two houses in one week. The whole experience was an eye-opening one for all of us.

And yet, even in this unplanned and underserviced area, one could see the basic requirements of New Urbanism in place. We were housed in an orphanage that was connected to the church in the center of the neighborhood. Within a five-minute walk one could find all of the necessary goods and services needed for daily living. All of the commercial buildings were centrally located, and twice a week a market was held on the main street. While walking to a particular destination, we had plenty of opportunity for greeting and conversing with local residents. The houses were by no means luxurious, but they were individually designed and built and reflected the distinct personality of their owners. Even the houses that were built by an outside group according to a standard template (as we had done) had fairly quickly adapted to their owners' personality. Whatever formal beauty that was lacking in the individual houses was made up for by the beauty and elegance of the central church.

I am not romanticizing the slums of Tijuana as in any way providing an exemplary or even adequate quality of life for those who have no choice but to live there. We saw abject poverty, unsanitary conditions, and insufficient medical services in every direction. And there were certainly not any planned or beautiful public spaces for residents to relax and be reminded of their dignity. Undoubtedly, in the slums of Tijuana, there continues to be a desperate need for major government assistance and investment.

My point is simply that when economic resources are restricted, humanity tends to arrange itself according to New Urbanist principles rather than suburban ones. We need to keep in mind that it has been our wealth and power—not our poverty—that has led us to the suburban sprawl model of development. And it will be much more resource-effective (both financially and environmentally) if we can somehow relearn how to function in an urban setting.

I do believe that once zoning laws are changed and the market corrects itself according to the renewed interest in urbanism, we will see a marked decrease in the cost of living and an increase in the quality of life for everybody. But this is a long-term goal, and it may take some time before we get there. We can be sure that in the meantime there will be minor (and major) injustices that we encounter along the way. Because the government has been slow to respond to the New Urbanists' appeals, much of their success has been market-driven. The market can be an effective, but cruel, mechanism of social change. Gentrification will renew and restore some very dilapidated areas of our historic cities, but it also has the potential for displacing a great number of current residents of these areas as it does so.

As the New Urbanist movement continues along in this market-driven phase, it will be increasingly important for public Christians to keep justice considerations in the forefront of our minds. There are mechanisms that could allow residents of gentrifying areas who want to stay in their current neighborhoods to do so. And there are ways to integrate dignified low-income housing options into traditionally wealthier parts of town. We will need public Christians to flesh out these kinds of solutions and to encourage our advocacy of them. Already there are Christian groups that are equipped to head up such efforts. Groups like Habitat for Humanity, Mendenhall Ministries, and the Inner City Christian Federation of Grand Rapids have established a track record for providing good housing and have gained trust in the communities in which they operate. They most certainly could be important players as we try to sort out a humane approach to adopting urbanist principles.

■ Are We of Any Use?

As we've already demonstrated, New Urbanism is on the move. The market is responding to its insights, and even the government is slowly getting on board. There are a number of books, from a wide range of disciplines, that eloquently and effectively demonstrate the principles of New Urbanism. There are even a variety of journals devoted exclusively to the New Urbanist cause. My final question, then, has to do with whether the church has any distinct role to play in this movement. We saw in the introduction that the fact that the pastors of the church can have a meeting in a neighborhood coffee shop is not insignificant to the life and mission of the church. But does the church's presence in the daily life of the neighborhood ultimately have any bearing on the city as a cultural phenomenon?

We've already noted a need for Christians to redouble their efforts at evangelism in this renewed urban context. And we've noted the need for Christians to be increasingly vigilant with regard to justice concerns as New Urbanism affects residential patterns in this country. But those issues are really on "our turf" as it were. It is for the explicit benefit of the kingdom of God that we would pursue these ends. This is not to denigrate their importance in any way—serving the kingdom is our highest calling. However, it is worth taking a moment to consider whether the church has anything to offer the New Urbanists on "their turf."

I can think of a few resources that we might be able to offer the New Urbanist movement as a church. The first is that we are the stewards of some very important and useful public spaces within most urban areas. Historic churches represent some of the most beautiful and graceful landmarks in the heart of our cities. And they continue to provide viable public gathering spaces for all kinds of neighborhood groups. Our church, in addition to being an important historic landmark, provides a meeting place for a community-wide Persons with Disabilities Bible Study, the Boy

162

Scouts, the Riverside Neighborhood Council, and the Missoula County Public Schools Music Department—to name just a few groups.

In the forthcoming book *The Quiet Voice of God,*[1] Robert Wuthnow makes the point that churches may represent some of the last noncommercial public spaces in this country and thus may play an important role in the renewal of our civic life. This seems to be already happening quite spontaneously and without too much conscious effort on the part of congregations. However, as congregations become aware of the importance of this role, they can continue to work to improve their ability to play the role well.

Unfortunately, many congregations have already abandoned (or are giving serious consideration to abandoning) these important urban settings for the greener pastures of the suburbs. Before we consider the implications of this pattern, I will reiterate an earlier point. As long we have people moving to and living in the suburbs, we will need churches in the suburbs to serve those people's needs. However, doing effective ministry in the suburbs does not have to involve abandoning our urban church buildings. Urban churches are important (if often overlooked) anchors in the city. We may need to rethink how we use these buildings to be more effective as congregations, but we should at the very least hold onto them.

A second way that the church can benefit the New Urbanist movement is with its theological wisdom. The New Urbanist movement has helped to shift the architectural and planning professions away from functioning in an abstract and authoritarian manner. New Urbanists are in favor of architects and planners listening to the people whom they serve, so that their work can better reflect those people's values and aspirations. The fact of the matter is that the American public has been, and continues to be, a deeply religious people. Any attempt to develop an "architecture of community" that ignores the religious values that are deeply formative for that community is destined to be flawed. We still need to respect the separation of church and state, and we should not seek preferential treatment for our Christian tradition. But at some level, the ways that congregations understand and use the physical spaces of communities ought to have some bearing on the design of those communities. And the church can play an important role in clarifying and communicating that distinct voice in the public realm.

The New Urbanists may also want to hear from the Christian community about our doctrine of sin. I mean this in all sincerity. Any attempt to understand our patterns of sprawl and private consumption that fails to deal honestly with the human condition of sin is going to miss the mark. As G. K. Chesterton claimed, the doctrine of original sin is "the only part of Christian theology that can really be proved."[2] Chesterton made this observation from an early-twentieth-century English perspective, but anyone who has observed our American culture over the past century could come to the same conclusion. Even James Howard Kunstler (who is not a religious person) observes in his coda, "I begin to come to the disquieting conclusion that we Americans are these days a wicked people who deserve to be punished."[3] Perhaps we can help the New Urbanists better understand this insight, so that they can make wiser policy-level decisions. In reintroducing the concept of the reality of sin into the public arena, we may even find some new opportunities to share the good news about the stronger reality of grace. After all, people often will not have the courage to face up to their sin until they are assured about the good news of grace.

The last way that Christians might be able to contribute to the New Urbanist movement is through direct political involvement. Ever since the Scopes trial, the Christian community has been divided into two distinct and somewhat ineffective political camps. The Left has taken up some noble but impossibly huge issues, like third world debt forgiveness, and contented itself to be a prophetic, but easily overlooked, player on the political scene. The Right stayed out of politics for some time and then quickly reemerged in the 1980s with a somewhat random and disparate agenda of school prayer, tax cuts for families, and opposition to abortion. The Right has been somewhat more effective in winning political victories than has the Left, but it has done so by a raw exertion of power. There has been little in the way of genuine political engagement or civic dialogue, and as a result, the Right has just about worn out its welcome in the public eye.

I think that we could recover some effectiveness and community respect if the Christian community, both Left and Right, would take Daniel Kemmis's advice and turn our attention to politics at a municipal level. Our political agenda for specific issues needs to grow out of some coherent vision of what we understand the good life to look like.[4] And the city is the appropriate place to begin shaping that vision. The national arena is, and will continue to be, an important place for our voice to be heard. But we need to relearn the gracious art of politics on a local level.

We could begin by praying for municipal issues as well as for our civic leaders. In doing so we invite the Lord to help shape our vision, and we fulfill Paul's command to pray for our leaders. I find praying for local leaders to be particularly meaningful, because I can pray for them as individuals whom I know as well as for their families, with whom I interact.[5] When our prayers for leaders can include both policy issues as well as personal concerns, an important step in the healing of our political life has already been taken.[6]

I also believe that prayer often compels us to action. Once our minds become enlightened to the impact that civic issues have on our lives and our ministries, and once our hearts become engaged through prayer, we will find all kinds of ways for direct involvement. And this is all the more true when our prayers focus on local issues. We have to expend quite a bit of political capital to exert some kind of Christian influence at the national level. But at the municipal level, there is an openness to and appreciation of hard work and leadership from anyone who is willing to jump in.

It may come as some surprise that your city in many ways functions like your church—20 percent of the people do 80 percent of the work. Cities, like churches, relegate much of their work to committees of overworked volunteers and are almost always open to fresh involvement. Whether you live in a historic city and want to make sure that poor people aren't displaced by gentrification or you live in a suburb and would like to see a coffee shop in your subdivision, municipal politics provide an appropriate setting to advocate these views. I caution against trying to harness your whole Christian community to support the "Christian position" on most of these issues. Politics is, after all, messy business, and on most issues there are many opportunities for sincere Christians to disagree. But that doesn't mean that we cannot advocate passionately for issues from our own sense of Christian conviction and even attempt to form mini-coalitions to support our cause.

In a more general sense, we Christians could do a much better job of advocating for the basic value of citizenship. Voting in elections and serving on jury duty are important services that we render to our cities and larger communities. Getting to know our neighbors and taking responsibility for those with special needs in our neighborhoods are also part of our mandate as citizens. Citizenship means being a contributor to your society and not just a taxpayer who pays for a service.[7] And citizenship is ultimately what cities are all about. The earliest Christian community had the public reputation of "praising God and having the goodwill of all the people" (Acts 2:47). Perhaps we can learn to achieve both of these distinctions within a context of the city.

■ Christian Urbanism

After reading about the New Urbanism and being convinced that I could endorse the goals of this movement, I finally decided to join the Congress of the New Urbanism and become a card-carrying member. I called their office in San Francisco and had them send me an application. After filling out all of the information about myself, I saw a list of vocational categories from which I was to select the one that best applied to my situation. There were about twenty categories listed, including architect, builder, city planner, and government official. But there was no place to indicate that I was a pastor or a member of a religious community. I decided that I was best represented by the category of "other," scribbled in the title "Rev." before my name, and sent in my application.

I later called the congress back and asked why they hadn't provided a place to indicate involvement in a religious community on the application. I was told that there hadn't really been that much interest in their movement from the Christian community. I found myself wanting to explain that it was the Christian community that provided the vision behind so many of our great cities, that it is Christians who are currently at the forefront of serving those who live in cities, and that Christians manage some of the best civic spaces in most of our historic cities. I wanted to say that members of religious communities ought, if only for honorary reasons, to have their own category on the application. But I checked myself—realizing that irrespective of the principle involved, it just doesn't make sense to provide a category for "member of religious community" if there is no one who is going to select that category. And so I decided to let it go. What I did say was, "Please note somewhere that a Christian has joined your organization, and you should expect that more will follow."

I sincerely hope that within a few years there will be others who join the Congress for the New Urbanism on the basis of their Christian convictions. And I do hope that in time we will have our own category in the congress. Whether that happens or not, and whether the current movement known as New Urbanism amounts to anything or not, I am quite sure that the Christian community in this country will eventually come around to fulfilling its role as city people. I am confident in this because I know about the New Jerusalem, and I also know that our current relation to heaven is described as "citi-zenship." For those who can learn to appreciate and love the city now—so much the better. And for those who can't? Well, they'll just have a lot of catching up to do.

Appendix A: City Words — A Constructive Glossary

Built environment The buildings, infrastructure, landscaping, and in-between places that we create for ourselves. Unlike our natural environment, our built environment can be very beautiful or very ugly. Like our natural environment, however, our built environment (especially the beautiful parts) can be fragile and even irreplaceable. Our historic downtowns are a little like old-growth forests: we may destroy them because of neglect, but if we do, we will not be able to replace them quickly.

Charrette A community-wide visioning event that can be used to break deadlocks on controversial issues and to free up creative problem solving. A charrette can be a day-long or a week-long meeting in which participants agree to "check their guns at the door" and to work together in small groups until they come up with some workable solutions. A charrette typically includes experts, stakeholders, and residents of a particular area.

Citizen Literally, a denizen of or dweller in the *city*. Citizens actively participate in governing themselves. Being a citizen is more than merely being a taxpayer giving money and receiving services. Every type of government has taxpayers; only a democracy has citizens. Good cities foster good citizens.

Civic art The design and planning of cities that goes beyond utilitarian concerns such as safety, parking, and traffic flow, but rather reflects the values and aspirations of a community. Civic art can accentuate major public buildings by placing them at the terminus of major streets or by allowing them to be built higher than the other buildings on the skyline. Civic art can regulate building materials and architectural style to preserve a city's identity. Civic art does not attempt to supplant the role of the individual architects, but interprets the meaning of the city for the architects.

167

Community A group of people living in the same locality under the same government. We have almost lost the local aspect of this word and instead use it to describe groups with shared interests: gay community, Christian community, etc. A community should first and foremost consist of our neighbors.

Compassion Deep awareness of the suffering of another, coupled with the wish to relieve it. One implication of extreme-separation zoning laws is that they reduce our contact with people of other socioeconomic classes and thus reduce our potential for compassion.

Context The surrounding environment (natural, architectural, or historical). A new building should be neither a minimalist structure nor a monument to the architect; it should fit in with the other buildings in the area and with the natural features of the landscape.

Corridor A physical feature that provides a link between various parts of a city. A corridor can be a natural feature such as a river or it can be a constructed feature such as railroad tracks or a walking path.

Critical mass A sufficient number of people to engage in or sustain meaningful conversation or action around a specific topic or concern. Many of the great political, cultural, and scientific advancements have taken place in cities because of critical mass.

Density Numbers of dwellings per acre of land. *High density* is often confused with *overcrowding,* which means "too many people in a dwelling for the number of rooms it contains." Overcrowding is a public nuisance; high density can actually be very good for a city. Some of the highest-rent areas in the world contain high densities.

Dialogue An informal exchange of views. It appears that we are losing the ability as a culture to engage in dialogue, and instead forming camps and constituencies and hurling words at one another without mutually seeking truth. What is missing is any real relationship with an "other." We reduce another to a label rather than seeing a person. The public life of cities is meant to provide a venue for the exchange of views and the building of relationships.

Dignity The quality or state of being worthy of esteem or respect. Grand buildings evoke a sense of dignity not only for themselves, but also for the community that built and sustains them. Ugly buildings or standardized buildings lack dignity.

District An area of the city that remains single-use out of necessity within a New Urbanist approach to development. Heavy industry and institutional complexes like universities and hospitals often will require a singe-use district.

Gentrification The process by which private money is invested in dilapidated sections of the inner city, buildings are recycled for new uses, and property values tend to increase significantly. There is currently a debate over whether gentrification is a key to revitalizing the inner city or whether it forces the poor out of the inner city through higher housing costs.

Growth In cities, the discussion of growth tends to center around increases in population, the number of buildings, and traffic. Often the terms of the debate seem to imply that we can either allow growth or prevent growth at a policy level. In most cases, we cannot cause or prohibit growth, but can only decide between planned and unplanned growth.

Height In creating a feeling of enclosure (which is essential to a comfortable walking environment), building height is an important component: generally a ratio of at least 6:1 (ratio of distance from the front of one building to the one across the street to the height of the building). Many building codes that restrict height arbitrarily and have setback requirements often make achieving this ratio impossible.

History An awareness of history is one of the factors that roots us to our localities and to the people in our community. Buildings can provide important markers of the history of a community. Architecture that either ignores history (standardized plans) or rejects history (modernism) weakens our sense of community.

Human imprint A distinguishing influence or effect caused by the efforts of a particular individual. Buildings that are individually designed or construction that includes fine detail work have a human imprint. Buildings that have a human imprint give testimony to the dignity of hard work and preserve the value of the human spirit.

Human scale The elements that make a building or place relate to human size. The elements (doors, windows, trees, ceiling height) are of sizes that can be easily comprehended by the eye and seem accessible for human operation. Human scale does not feel too big or too small to an individual person and thus better reflects the human being as God's crowning work of creation (Gen. 1:26–31).

Infill The strategy of applying (or reapplying) New Urbanist principles to decaying areas in the inner city. Often, these areas already have many of the features that are valuable in the New Urbanist mindset. All that is needed is an investment of love, capital, and imagination to turn these areas into places of dignity and beauty.

Legibility The use of visual cues to communicate information about a building. Through architectural features, messages can be conveyed, such as: "this is a barn," "enter here," "this is important," "speak softly here." Modernist architecture tends to disregard legibility to make a point. Buildings that are constructed solely on the basis of bottom-line economics often ignore the traditions of architectural legibility in favor of maximizing square footage.

Local Of, relating to, or characteristic of a particular place. The local features of a place connect people to a place and to one another. With the advent of standardized buildings and chain stores, it is getting harder to make any local distinctions between Atlanta and Seattle, or any other city in America.

LULU Locally Undesirable Land Use. *LULU* refers to low-income housing, power plants, dumps, and other land uses that are necessary for the functioning of the city, but are not desired in anyone's neighborhood. The only fair way to deal with LULUs is to distribute them evenly throughout the city.

Mixed-use Having a variety of residential types (single-family and multi-family dwellings), commercial uses (coffee shops, dry cleaners, and groceries), and community features (libraries and parks). Areas of mixed use provide reasons for people to leave their houses and interact with their neighbors.

Neighborhood The basic building block of human community. Real neighborhoods tend to exist more in our popular imagination (Sesame Street) than in real life. One of the contributions of the New Urbanist movement has been to articulate five specific attributes of traditional neighborhood design (TND). They are (1) a center and edge; (2) a quarter mile from center to edge; (3) mixed use; (4) interconnecting streets; (5) priority to public spaces and civic buildings over private structures.

New Urbanism A movement of architects, builders, city planners, and lay persons that advocates development based upon principles of historic downtowns and traditional neighborhoods.

NORC Naturally Occurring Retirement Community. A neighborhood that has many of the amenities required for daily life within walking distance of residential homes. A person who lives in a NORC can discontinue driving and continue to live a full and independent life. Before 1950 NORCs were the norm; now they are fairly rare and consequently expensive to live in.

Outbuilding Any building that is separate from but associated with the main building on a lot. Outbuildings (or granny flats), where they are legal, provide one of the best options for low-income housing, and they provide one more option for keeping the elderly connected to our communities. Zoning codes that make the rental of out-buildings illegal needlessly limit a viable solution to low-income housing needs.

Pedestrian scale The design of a community that allows for or assumes that people will walk from place to place. Mixed-use neighborhoods and historic downtowns tend to have pedestrian scale. Pedestrian scale enhances the health of those who choose to walk, helps build relationships among people, and provides access to those who cannot drive a car (children and some elderly and handicapped people). Most postwar development has not only ignored pedestrian scale, but in many cases has made walking from place to place an impossibility.

Place An area of a particular quality with definite or indefinite boundaries. Place can be an important feature of our identity (Jesus of Nazareth, Paul of Tarsus). The standardization of our culture has reduced the significance of place and has contributed to a sense of rootlessness among our population.

Plaza Formerly, a hard-surfaced public square, often flanked by important and beautiful buildings in a city. In a disturbing development, the word *plaza* is now used to describe a style of low and featureless private building with almost no pedestrian interest. One would be hard-pressed to come up with another example of such antithetical concepts being described with the same word.

Preservation The act of keeping or remaining intact. Preservationists have focused on maintaining or restoring our historic areas to improve the quality of our built environments. Their work can be distinguished from that of the New Urbanists, who have focused on new developments based on old principles learned from cities.

Public space A place that is accessible for anyone to use. Sidewalks, plazas, and parks are the three most common public spaces. Public spaces mitigate class distinctions by allowing us to interact on neutral territory, and they foster relationships within a community by providing opportunities for incidental contact.

Quality A degree or grade of excellence. Older buildings tend to have a higher degree of quality than do newer ones. Quality in construction lends dignity to the builders of a particular building and indicates a long-term commitment to a community. The majority of current commercial buildings are of low quality and have an anticipated life span of only twenty to thirty years.

Reductionism The attempt to explain complex phenomena by relatively simple principles. Current economic theories based upon cost-benefit analysis tend to lead toward a certain kind of reductionism. Corporations as well as individuals are motivated to get the most product for the least amount of money in any transaction and tend to ignore issues of beauty, quality, and human relationship.

Setback The distance from the public right-of-way to the front of a building. Traditionally, deep setbacks were used to set apart grand public buildings and mansions to accentuate their importance to the community and to maximize their visibility. Currently, it is typical to have a standard minimum thirty-foot setback requirement for every building in a city. This is usually justified on the basis of parking needs, but it works completely against aesthetic and pedestrian considerations. Consider the layout of a typical K-Mart versus a traditional downtown, and you will get a sense of what kind of development our current setback laws are leading us to.

Sidewalk Sidewalks are often overlooked as public spaces but in actuality are more effective than parks or plazas in bringing people together and increasing the relational quality of our day-to-day life. Many new residential developments do not include sidewalks or do not provide a continuous walkway.

Smart growth The planning philosophy behind growth management plans that employ some New Urbanist principles. Obviously, it is a highly subjective term, and its meaning will vary considerably with each use. Not every policy that purports to encourage smart growth will truly employ New Urbanist principles.

Sprawl Haphazard growth or extension outward, especially that resulting from real estate development on the outskirts of a city. Sprawl is usually the default result of a lack of planned growth or the inability of a community to reach consensus about growth issues.

Stranger One who is neither a friend nor an acquaintance. As Christians we are called to be kind to strangers (Matthew 25). However, by emphasizing the private over the public, we have effectively eliminated strangers from our day-to-day life.

Streets There are two basic design strategies for streets. There is the traditional grid network, which is pedestrian-friendly and traffic-calming. And there is the cul-de-sac, collector-road style, which tends to bottleneck auto traffic around the collector roads and is unsafe and unfriendly to pedestrians.

TND Traditional Neighborhood Design; *see also* Neighborhood. Guidelines put forth by the New Urbanists. This approach to housing development is becoming increasingly popular and lucrative. The state of Wisconsin recently passed legislation to require TND development for towns of over twelve thousand in population. As its popularity increases, the danger will be that developers will try only to use the jargon.

Traffic calming The use of roadway geometry or physical structures to slow down automobile traffic and increase pedestrian safety. Traffic-calming devices have become very popular in Europe and are becoming more so in this country.

Twenty-four-hour city A city that is used by people continuously. It requires a mix of commercial and residential buildings for a wide range of income levels. A twenty-four-hour city enjoys a symbiotic relationship between safety and interest. It is interesting because all kinds of people can be found on its sidewalks and in its public spaces throughout the day. And it is safe because of the numbers of people out and about as well as watching the activity from their residential windows.

Urban renewal The strategy of improving slums by tearing down old buildings and putting up new, "improved" structures. It was the philosophy behind the Housing Act of 1949, which had disastrous results. Most of the "war-zone" housing projects in our inner cities are the result of urban renewal.

Zoning Designating a section of an area or a territory for a specific purpose or a particular type of building, enterprise, or activity. Most of our current zoning laws are based upon the faulty principle that separate activities need to take place in separate areas. This philosophy minimizes interaction among residential neighbors and virtually necessitates the use of the automobile to function in our society.

Appendix B: City Reading

■ Classics

Haworth, Lawrence
The Good City (Bloomington: Indiana University Press, 1963). One of the reasons that we have been unable to create a satisfying urban experience for ourselves as Americans is that we have resisted the notion that we are an urban nation; rather, we prefer to hang on nostalgically to an increasingly unrealistic rural dream. Professor Haworth's landmark book seeks above all to take the city seriously. He does not detest the city, as many of our intellectuals have done over the years, nor does he give in to the power of the city as an inevitable externality of progress. Instead, he seeks to explore ways that the city can continue to be a source of opportunity without at the same time destroying community.

Jacobs, Jane
The Death and Life of Great American Cities (New York: Vintage Books, 1961). Jane Jacobs is the patron saint of the New Urbanist movement. Over forty years old now, her *The Death and Life of Great American Cities* continues to provide a fresh and scintillating critique of our current building and zoning practices. From her three chapters on the uses of sidewalks, to her description of how a well-intentioned park can become a haven for perverts, to a chapter on how length of blocks affects the vibrancy of a neighborhood, Jacobs shows the vital importance of the seemingly ordinary features of our cities. I'm not aware of a single book in the New Urbanist canon that doesn't cite Jane Jacobs with reverent tones.

Whyte, William
The Last Landscape (Garden City, N.Y.: Doubleday, 1968). William Whyte is another writer who was well ahead of his time in understanding

how cities actually function and how to make them function even better. He and Jacobs share the distinct advantage of a certain level of humility and respect for historical contingency. Critical of utopian dreams in which the city is redrawn on a clean slate, Whyte advocates working with the organic patterns of life that happen within the city. Critical also of the decentralizing trends that continue to misinform most city planning, Whyte advocates keeping cities high-density but highly livable and vibrant settings for human habitation.

■ Philosophy

Borgmann, Albert

Crossing the Postmodern Divide (Chicago: University of Chicago Press, 1992). Picking up on some of the themes that he developed in his earlier book, *Technology and the Character of Modern Life,* Professor Borgmann here applies his framework to the problem of unexamined modernism that plagues contemporary life. In what is probably the most helpful guide to postmodernist culture, Borgmann shows the potential of a well-functioning city to bring out the best features of this intellectual movement. He describes the car and twenty-four-hour grocery stores as expressions of a modernist mindset and deeply destructive to the fabric of our cities. And he exalts the game of baseball and the sacrament of communion as helpful correctives to rampant modernism.

Kemmis, Daniel

The Good City and the Good Life: Renewing the Sense of Community (Boston: Houghton Mifflin, 1995). With a classics background, a law degree, and political experience as a state legislator and mayor of Missoula, Kemmis brings a unique voice to the New Urbanist conversation. He reminds us of the relatively simple and humane form that politics can take at the municipal level and calls us to a renewed commitment to being good citizens and good neighbors. With evocative images, such as that of the city as a vast stage (including the mayor cast as the buffoon) where we rehearse our communal stories, each chapter follows an intriguing thread: from ancient Athens, through Missoula, and on to international destinations such as Hong Kong and Neckargemund, Germany. Not one to be easily typecast into any movement, Kemmis provides depth and authenticity to the New Urbanist literature.

■ Architecture

Alexander, Christopher

The Timeless Way of Building (New York: Oxford University Press, 1979). In this work, Christopher Alexander develops the notion that designing and building structures to live and work in have been fundamental human activities throughout most of history that have provided us with identity and meaning. He believes that building practices have developed naturally, in a manner similar to language development. This natural process has been disrupted by highly specialized and nonlocal developers in many modern settings, and we are consequently losing a sense of architectural language.

Alexander, Christopher, Sara Ishakawa, and Murray Silverstein

A Pattern Language: Towns, Buildings, Construction (New York: Oxford University Press, 1977). In this work, Alexander tries to develop a primer for the architectural language that he introduces in *The Timeless Way of Building.* He identifies 253 distinct patterns that form the vocabulary for our architectural language. It sounds like an eccentric and abstract project until the reader stumbles across his convincing case for the advantages of divided-light windows over plateglass or the necessity of balconies being at least six feet deep. Even if you don't agree with his basic premise, you will be drawn in by his convincing maxims.

Duany, Andres, Elizabeth Plater-Zyberk, and Jeff Speck

Suburban Nation: The Rise of Sprawl and the Decline of the American Dream (New York: North Point Press, 2000). Having designed and implemented hundreds of New Urbanist developments throughout the country, Duany and Plater-Zyberk have established themselves as some of the most coherent and effective advocates of New Urbanism in this country. They not only have provided much of the foundational thinking for this movement from the field of architecture, they have led countless town meetings and charrettes on this subject, which gives them credibility with the nonspecialist. They provide enough technical explanation to allow the ordinary citizen to challenge such seemingly unassailable assertions as the ones that streets need to be wide for fire safety or that more lanes reduce traffic congestion. This book is probably the best expression of New Urbanist thinking.

Katz, Peter

The New Urbanism: Toward an Architecture of Community (New York: McGraw-Hill, 1994). This book begins with four introductory essays that outline some of the basic New Urbanist principles written by some of the pioneers in this field. It then examines twenty-four New

Urbanist case studies (both new and revitalization projects) to show how these principles work in concrete settings. The afterword, written by architectural historian Vincent Scully, puts this movement in historical perspective.

Lennard, Suzanne H. Crowhurst, and Henry L. Lennard

Livable Cities Observed: A Source Book of Images and Ideas (Carmel, Calif.: Gondolier Press, 1995). This book is put out by the International Making Cities Livable Council, a group committed to many of the same principles as those espoused by the Congress for the New Urbanism. Their scope is much more international than the CNU's, which makes some of their ideas somewhat less practical in an American context but provides some of the best examples of civic art, buildings, and public spaces in the world. This book makes a great companion volume to *Suburban Nation.*

Morrish, William R., and Catherine R. Brown

Planning to Stay: Learning to See the Physical Features of Your Neighborhood (Minneapolis: Milkweed Editions, 1994). This book is written by architects, but is intended to help nonspecialists to understand the features of their neighborhoods categorically. It then provides some models and resources for citizen activists to organize their neighbors for the purpose of improving their neighborhood.

Unwin, Raymond

Town Planning in Practice: An Introduction to the Art of Designing Cities and Suburbs (New York: Princeton Architectural Press, 1994). This book was originally published in 1909 and was reprinted in 1994 with an introduction by New Urbanist Andres Duany, "not as a memorial to its historical significance, but as a modern manual on technique." This book comes from an era when city planning was an art form, before it was abdicated to bureaucrats and traffic specialists.

■ Cultural Critique

Kunstler, James Howard

The Geography of Nowhere: The Rise and Decline of America's Man-Made Landscape (New York: Touchstone, 1993). James Howard Kunstler is the raving prophet of the New Urbanist movement. His narrative account of how we have gotten to our present state is part tragedy and part comedy, and always on target. He doesn't try to offer a balanced or fair account of the various forces that have contributed to our sprawling placelessness, but makes a convincing case nonetheless.

Home from Nowhere: Remaking Our Everyday World for the Twenty-First Century (New York: Touchstone, 1996). Three years after the publication of *The Geography of Nowhere,* a more hopeful Kunstler finds places where the idea of quality community life is making a comeback. His scathing critique continues to lurk in the background as he contrasts his good discoveries with ironic examples of "the world's highest standard of living."

Langdon, Philip

A Better Place to Live: Reshaping the American Suburb (Amherst: University of Massachusetts Press, 1994). Philip Langdon helped to put New Urbanism on the map with his 1988 *Atlantic Monthly* article on Andres Duany and Elizabeth Plater-Zyberk. He was so taken by his subject that he just kept writing, and this fine contribution to the New Urbanist canon was the result. Langdon's book is particularly helpful on the refurbishing of failed suburban developments (also known as brownfield development).

Moe, Richard, and Carter Wilkie

Changing Places: Rebuilding Community in the Age of Sprawl (New York: Henry Holt, 1997). This is an important book from the preservationist perspective. Preservationists were initially skeptical of the New Urbanist movement for its interest in building traditional neighborhoods on green space when we already have many traditional neighborhoods that are dying for lack of investment. These two movements have more recently discovered the symbiotic role that they can play for one another.

Pindell, Terry

A Good Place to Live: America's Last Migration (New York: Henry Holt, 1995). Terry Pindell explores his thesis that we Americans are a restless lot—constantly on the move looking for something better—by examining sixteen cities that seem to offer the kind of quality of life that the recent wave of migrants are looking for. These cities, of course, are the ones that have avoided the pitfalls of extreme-separation zoning and municipal policies that give the car priority over the pedestrian.

■ History

Jackson, Kenneth T.

Crabgrass Frontier: The Suburbanization of the United States (New York: Oxford University Press, 1985). This is the definitive history of the many and complex forces that have led to the sprawling and segregated existence that we have carved out for ourselves over the past two hundred years. Kenneth Jackson is a thorough and careful scholar who doesn't say more than he can demonstrate with solid evidence.

Rybczynski, Witold

City Life (New York: Touchstone, 1995). Another good history of cities and how ours got to be the way they are. His scope goes back farther than Jackson's and is more international. But Rybczynski too is a careful and fair scholar. If he has strong opinions about what should be or how we should get there, he keeps them in the background.

■ Sociology

Oldenburg, Ray

The Great Good Place: Cafés, Coffee Shops, Community Centers, Beauty Parlors, General Stores, Bars, Hangouts, and How They Get You through the Day (New York: Paragon House, 1989). Ray Oldenburg coined the term "third place," which has captured the imagination of our popular culture. Everyone needs a place between the work environment and home to relax and let off steam. He makes a good case for how such third places not only offer a viable substitute for a large house with every possible amenity, but actually provide many things that even the most lavish private sphere cannot. He finds confirmation of this theory everywhere from Midwestern rural truck stops to urbane European cafés.

Putnam, Robert D.

Bowling Alone: The Collapse and Revival of American Community (New York: Simon and Schuster, 2000). Putnam defines *social capital* as a tangible productive asset, comparable to physical capital and human capital. He asserts that we have lost a great deal of social capital in this country over the past half-century and are paying a cost in legal fees and security costs. One significant factor (not the most significant factor) in this loss has been the increased time that we spend in the automobile as a result of our sprawling residential patterns.

Appendix C: Charter of the New Urbanism

■ The Congress for the New Urbanism views disinvestment in central cities, the spread of placeless sprawl, increasing separation by race and income, environmental deterioration, loss of agricultural lands and wilderness, and the erosion of society's built heritage as one interrelated community-building challenge.

We stand for the restoration of existing urban centers and towns within coherent metropolitan regions, the reconfiguration of sprawling suburbs into communities of real neighborhoods and diverse districts, the conservation of natural environments, and the preservation of our built legacy.

We recognize that physical solutions by themselves will not solve social and economic problems, but neither can economic vitality, community stability, and environmental health be sustained without a coherent and supportive physical framework.

We advocate the restructuring of public policy and development practices to support the following principles: neighborhoods should be diverse in use and population; communities should be designed for the pedestrian and transit as well as the car; cities and towns should be shaped by physically defined and universally accessible public spaces and community institutions; urban places should be framed by architecture and landscape design that celebrate local history, climate, ecology, and building practice.

We represent a broad-based citizenry, composed of public and private sector leaders, community activists, and multidisciplinary professionals. We are committed to reestablishing the relationship between the art of building and the making of community, through citizen-based participatory planning and design.

We dedicate ourselves to reclaiming our homes, blocks, streets, parks, neighborhoods, districts, towns, cities, regions, and environment. We assert the following principles to guide public policy, development practice, urban planning, and design:

■ The Region: Metropolis, City, and Town

1. Metropolitan regions are finite places with geographic boundaries derived from topography, watersheds, coastlines, farmlands, regional parks, and river basins. The metropolis is made of multiple centers that are cities, towns, and villages, each with its own identifiable center and edges.
2. The metropolitan region is a fundamental economic unit of the contemporary world. Governmental cooperation, public policy, physical planning, and economic strategies must reflect this new reality.
3. The metropolis has a necessary and fragile relationship to its agrarian hinterland and natural landscapes. The relationship is environmental, economic, and cultural. Farmland and nature are as important to the metropolis as the garden is to the house.
4. Development patterns should not blur or eradicate the edges of the metropolis. Infill development within existing urban areas conserves environmental resources, economic investment, and social fabric, while reclaiming marginal and abandoned areas. Metropolitan regions should develop strategies to encourage such infill development over peripheral expansion.
5. Where appropriate, new development contiguous to urban boundaries should be organized as neighborhoods and districts, and be integrated with the existing urban pattern. Noncontiguous development should be organized as towns and villages with their own urban edges, and planned for a jobs/housing balance, not as bedroom suburbs.
6. The development and redevelopment of towns and cities should respect historical patterns, precedents, and boundaries.
7. Cities and towns should bring into proximity a broad spectrum of public and private uses to support a regional economy that benefits people of all incomes. Affordable housing should be distributed throughout the region to match job opportunities and to avoid concentrations of poverty.
8. The physical organization of the region should be supported by a framework of transportation alternatives. Transit, pedestrian, and

bicycle systems should maximize access and mobility throughout the region while reducing dependence upon the automobile.

9. Revenues and resources can be shared more cooperatively among the municipalities and centers within regions to avoid destructive competition for tax base and to promote rational coordination of transportation, recreation, public services, housing, and community institutions.

■ The Neighborhood, the District, and the Corridor

1. The neighborhood, the district, and the corridor are the essential elements of development and redevelopment in the metropolis. They form identifiable areas that encourage citizens to take responsibility for their maintenance and evolution.
2. Neighborhoods should be compact, pedestrian-friendly, and mixed-use. Districts generally emphasize a special single use, and should follow the principles of neighborhood design when possible. Corridors are regional connectors of neighborhoods and districts; they range from boulevards and rail lines to rivers and parkways.
3. Many activities of daily living should occur within walking distance, allowing independence to those who do not drive, especially the elderly and the young. Interconnected networks of streets should be designed to encourage walking, reduce the number and length of automobile trips, and conserve energy.
4. Within neighborhoods, a broad range of housing types and price levels can bring people of diverse ages, races, and incomes into daily interaction, strengthening the personal and civic bonds essential to an authentic community.
5. Transit corridors, when properly planned and coordinated, can help organize metropolitan structure and revitalize urban centers. In contrast, highway corridors should not displace investment from existing centers.
6. Appropriate building densities and land uses should be within walking distance of transit stops, permitting public transit to become a viable alternative to the automobile.
7. Concentrations of civic, institutional, and commercial activity should be embedded in neighborhoods and districts, not isolated in remote, single-use complexes. Schools should be sized and located to enable children to walk or bicycle to them.

8. The economic health and harmonious evolution of neighborhoods, districts, and corridors can be improved through graphic urban design codes that serve as predictable guides for change.
9. A range of parks, from tot-lots and village greens to ball fields and community gardens, should be distributed within neighborhoods. Conservation areas and open lands should be used to define and connect different neighborhoods and districts.

■ The Block, the Street, and the Building

1. A primary task of all urban architecture and landscape design is the physical definition of streets and public spaces as places of shared use.
2. Individual architectural projects should be seamlessly linked to their surroundings. This issue transcends style.
3. The revitalization of urban places depends on safety and security. The design of streets and buildings should reinforce safe environments, but not at the expense of accessibility and openness.
4. In the contemporary metropolis, development must adequately accommodate automobiles. It should do so in ways that respect the pedestrian and the form of public space.
5. Streets and squares should be safe, comfortable, and interesting to the pedestrian. Properly configured, they encourage walking and enable neighbors to know each other and protect their communities.
6. Architecture and landscape design should grow from local climate, topography, history, and building practice.
7. Civic buildings and public gathering places require important sites to reinforce community identity and the culture of democracy. They deserve distinctive form, because their role is different from that of other buildings and places that constitute the fabric of the city.
8. All buildings should provide their inhabitants with a clear sense of location, weather and time. Natural methods of heating and cooling can be more resource efficient than mechanical systems.
9. Preservation and renewal of historic buildings, districts, and landscapes affirm the continuity and evolution of urban society.

Notes

Introduction

1. Daniel Kemmis, *The Good City and the Good Life* (New York: Houghton Mifflin, 1995), 21.

2. Ibid., 24.

3. Ibid., 48.

4. Jane Jacobs, *The Death and Life of Great American Cities* (1961; reprint, New York: Vintage Books, 1992).

5. James Howard Kunstler, *The Geography of Nowhere: The Rise and Decline of America's Man-Made Landscape* (New York: Simon & Schuster, 1993); and *Home from Nowhere: Remaking Our Everyday World for the 21st Century* (New York: Simon & Schuster, 1998).

6. See Peter Katz, *The New Urbanism: Toward an Architecture of Community* (New York: McGraw Hill, 1994); and Richard Moe and Carter Wilkie, *Changing Places: Rebuilding Community in the Age of Sprawl* (New York: Henry Holt and Co., 1997).

7. Revelation 21:2.

Chapter 1

1. *American Heritage Dictionary of the English Language,* 3d ed., s.v. "individualism."

2. Mark 5:30–34.

3. Abraham Kuyper, "Uniformity: The Curse of Modern Life," in *Abraham Kuyper: A Centennial Reader*, ed. James D. Bratt (Grand Rapids: Eerdmans, 1998), 26.

4. Ibid.

5. Andres Duany, Elizabeth Plater-Zyberk, and Jeff Speck, *Suburban Nation: The Rise of Sprawl and the Decline of the American Dream* (New York: North Point Press, 2000), 123.

6. Christopher Alexander, *A Pattern Language: Towns, Buildings, Construction* (New York: Oxford University Press, 1977), 216–17.

7. Genesis 2:18.

8. Exodus 7:1; 18:13–23.

9. 1 Corinthians 12:14–26.

10. Alexander, *A Pattern Language*, 142–43.

11. The connection between these events is made more fully by Kunstler, *Home from Nowhere*, 42.

12. Ibid., 43.

13. Exodus 12:33.

14. Daniel 6:23.

15. Philemon 1:17.

16. Romans 6:16–17.

17. The Dwight D. Eisenhower Library <www.eisenhower.utexas.edu/content.htm>.

18. *Statistical Abstract of the United States: 2001,* Washington D.C.: U.S. Department of Commerce, Table 1083.

19. Kenneth T. Jackson, *Crabgrass Frontier: The Suburbanization of the United States* (New York: Oxford University Press, 1985), 170.

20. Ibid.

21. Ibid., 203.

22. John G. Mitchell, "Urban Sprawl," in *National Geographic,* July 2001.

23. *Village of Euclid* v. *Ambler Realty Co.,* 272 U.S. 365 (1926).

Chapter 2

1. *American Heritage Dictionary,* 3d ed., s.v. "annex."

2. "City Over Exerts Its Power," letter to the editor, *Missoulian,* October 4, 2001.

3. Genesis 4:14.

4. Ibid.

5. Genesis 10:8.

6. Genesis 11:4.

7. Exodus 1:11.

8. Jacques Ellul, *The Meaning of the City,* trans. Dennis Pardee (Grand Rapids: Eerdmans, 1970), 41.

9. Deuteronomy 6:10.

10. Leviticus 14:40.

11. Leviticus 15:31.

12. Numbers 35:10–12.

13. 2 Samuel 5:1–5.

14. 2 Samuel 5:12.

15. John Bright, *A History of Israel,* 3d ed. (Philadelphia: Westminster Press, 1981), 201.

16. Deuteronomy 16:15.

17. 2 Samuel 7:10.

18. 2 Samuel 7:12–13.

19. 1 Kings 8:16.

20. 1 Kings 9:3.

21. Psalms 122:1–2; 125:2.

22. Isaiah 33:20.

23. Isaiah 1:21.

24. Christopher Seitz, "The Two Cities in Christian Scripture," in *The Two Cities of God: The Church's Responsibility for the Earthly City,* ed. Carl E. Braaten and Robert W. Jenson (Grand Rapids: Eerdmans, 1997), 13.

25. Revelation 21:2.

26. Philippians 3:20.

27. Kemmis, *Good City,* 9.

28. Genesis 50:20.

Chapter 3

1. Romans 15:23.

2. Martin Marty quotes Josiah Strong's use of these terms and then develops them more fully in Martin E. Marty, *Righteous Empire: The Protestant Experience in America* (New York: Dial Press: 1970), 177–87.

3. J. I. Packer in the foreword to Craig M. Gay, *The Way of the (Modern) World: Or, Why It's Tempting to Live As If God Doesn't Exist* (Grand Rapids: Eerdmans, 1998), ix.

4. George M. Marsden, *Fundamentalism and American Culture: The Shaping of Twentieth-Century Evangelicalism, 1870–1925* (Oxford: Oxford University Press, 1980), 92.

5. Ibid., 185.

6. Ibid., 186.

7. David F. Wells, *No Place for Truth:* Or, *Whatever Happened to Evangelical Theology?* (Grand Rapids: Eerdmans, 1993), 183.

8. Martin E. Marty, *Righteous Empire,* 179.

9. Martin E. Marty, "Religion, Politics, and Family," public lecture, 12th Mansfield Conference, University of Montana, 1996.

10. Albert Borgmann, *Crossing the Postmodern Divide* (Chicago: University of Chicago Press, 1992),122.

11. Ibid., 125.

12. Ibid., 128.

13. Ibid., 130.

14. Ibid., 131.

15. Ibid., 134.

16. Kemmis, *Good City,* 6.

17. Ibid., 20.

18. Ibid., 21.

Chapter 4

1. John 1:14.

2. John 20.

3. 1 Corinthians 15:20.

4. Philippians 3:19.

5. Matthew 11:19.

6. Revelation 21:2.

7. Genesis 9:10; Exodus 20:10; Deuteronomy 20:19.

8. Romans 8:21.

9. Hebrews 13:14

10. Revelation. 21:4.

11. Jeremiah 29:7.

12. Galatians 5:22.

13. Quoted in Moe and Wilkie, *Changing Places*, 13.

Chapter 5

1. Daniel Kemmis, personal interview, April 2000.

2. John 1:14.

3. There is an interesting legal case that is relevant to this issue. In 1979 the California Supreme Court decided in favor of Michael Robins against Pruneyard Shopping Center that an individual does have the right to use a privately owned shopping center to solicit signatures for a petition not directly related to commercial purposes. This is, of course, a contested ruling, and this kind of behavior continues to be prohibited at many malls.

4. Jacobs, *Death and Life of Great American Cities.*

Chapter 6

1. Katz, *New Urbanism*, xviii.

2. Matthew 9:18–26.

3. Ray Oldenburg, *The Great Good Place: Cafés, Coffee Shops, Community Centers, Beauty Parlors, General Stores, Bars, Hangouts, and How They Get You through the Day* (New York: Paragon House, 1989).

4. Robert Putnam, *Bowling Alone: The Collapse and Revival of American Community* (New York: Simon and Schuster, 2000).

5. Psalms 1:1.

6. Psalms 15:2.

7. Micah 6:8.

8. 1 John 1:6–7.

9. Luke 24:32.

10. 2 Corinthians 5:7.

11. Robert Banks and R. Paul Stevens, eds., *The Complete Book of Everyday Christianity: An A-to-Z Guide to Following Christ in Every Aspect of Life* (Downers Grove, Ill.: InterVarsity Press, 1997), 1098.

12. Duany, Plater-Zyberk, and Speck, *Suburban Nation*, 78.

13. Betty Edwards, *The New Drawing on the Right Side of the Brain,* 2d ed. (New York: Jeremy P. Tarcher/Putnam, 1999).

Chapter 7

1. Psalm 19:1.
2. Exodus 26:31–32.
3. Exodus 36:1
4. Matthew 29:51.
5. I am indebted to Professor Christopher Miller of Judson College for helping me to find this term.
6. Proverbs 3:34; James 4:6.
7. Proverbs 13:10; 28:25
8. Joshua 4:1–9.
9. Exodus 13:3; Luke 22:19.
10. Proverbs 1:8–9.
11. Matthew 26:9
12. Ironically, modernists would in time create their own deceptions. The rough look became such a deliberate style that the exteriors of many modernist buildings have glued-on steel beams that are in no way integral to the structure.
13. Francis D. K. Ching, *A Visual Dictionary of Architecture* (New York: Wiley, 1995), 9.
14. Missoula Historic Preservation Advisory Commission et al., *Historic Missoula Montana*, 1993.
15. Kunstler, *Home from Nowhere*, 217.
16. I am indebted to Peter Lambros for this observation.
17. Missoula Historic Preservation Advisory Commission et al., *Historic Missoula Montana*.
18. Winston Churchill, speech to the House of Commons, October 28, 1943.
19. Definition provided by architect Lynn Schreuder.
20. Genesis 1:26–31.
21. Ephesians 6:7.
22. Philippians 4:8.

Chapter 8

1. 2 Timothy 3:14–15
2. Suzanne H. Crowhurst Lennard and Henry L. Lennard, *Livable Cities Observed: A Source Book of Images and Ideas* (Carmel, Calif.: Gondolier Press, 1995).
3. However, we noted in the last chapter that public buildings are doing that less and less.
4. Kemmis, *Good City*, 5.
5. Albert Borgmann, *Technology and the Character of Contemporary Life* (Chicago: University of Chicago Press, 1984), 236–42.
6. Ibid., 241.
7. Ibid.

Chapter 9

1. Sherry Devlin, Thomas Bauer, and John Engen, *A Carousel for Missoula: How a Town Came Together to Help a Man Build a Dream* (Missoula: The Missoulian, 1995), 4–11.
2. *The American Heritage Dictionary,* 2d ed., s.v. "critical mass."
3. Acts 16:11–15.
4. Revelation 1:11.
5. Philippians 4:9.
6. Jacobs, *Death and Life of Great American Cities,* 205.

Chapter 10

1. Matthew 25:34–40.
2. *Microsoft Word Encarta Dictionary,* s.v. "civility."
3. Jacobs, *Death and Life of Great American Cities*, 35.
4. Ibid., 171.
5. Reuben Greenberg (Chief of Police, Charleston, S.C.), *New Urban Post,* October 2001, 2.
6. Duany, Plater-Zyberk, and Speck, *Suburban Nation,* 146–47.

Conclusion

1. Cited in Charles T. Mathewes, "Reconsidering the Role of Mainline Churches in Public Life" *Theology Today* (January 2002), 554–56.
2. Gilbert K. Chesterton, *Orthodoxy* (Garden City, N.Y.: Doubleday Image, 1959), 15.
3. Kunstler, *Home from Nowhere*, 297.
4. One fruitful place to begin our search for such an integrated vision would be the writings of Abraham Kuyper.
5. An interesting sidenote to the conclusion of chapter five: after praying for sidewalks on Brooks Street for some time, I later came to discover that one of the people behind these sidewalks was Bruce Bender, who is the head of Missoula's Public Works Department. Bruce is the husband of Mari Bender, who is my daughter Kate's preschool teacher. And they are both active members of the Catholic parish down the street.
6. Incidentally, this kind of bipartisan prayer and support is already going on at the national, state, and county levels through the work of the International Foundation. This group puts on the National Prayer Breakfast and encourages informal Christian fellowship between political and business leaders.
7. Kemmis, *Good City,* 9.

For further information about the Congress for the New Urbansim:

Congress for the New Urbanism
5 Third Street, Suite 725
San Francisco, CA 94103
Phone: (415) 495-2255
Fax: (415) 495-1731

For further information about *Sidewalks in the Kingdom* or to download discussion questions for your study group:
www.brazospress.com\resources